Sew Many STARS
Techniques & Patterns

Gail Searl

American Quilter's Society

P. O. Box 3290 • Paducah, KY 42002-3290

Located in Paducah, Kentucky, the American Quilter's Society (AQS) is dedicated to promoting the accomplishments of today's quilters. Through its publications and events, AQS strives to honor today's quiltmakers and their work and to inspire future creativity and innovation in quiltmaking.

EDITOR: BARBARA SMITH
TECHNICAL EDITOR: BONNIE K. BROWNING
BOOK DESIGN/ILLUSTRATIONS: ELAINE WILSON
COVER DESIGN: MICHAEL BUCKINGHAM
PHOTOGRAPHY: CHARLES R. LYNCH

Library of Congress Cataloging-in-Publication Data
Gail Searl
     Sew many stars : techniques & patterns / Gail Searl.
               p.   cm.
     ISBN 1-57432-715-1
     1. Patchwork--Patterns. 2. Machine quilting--Patterns. 3. Stars in art. I. Title: Stars. II. Title.

TT835 .S42 1999
746.46041--dc21   99-048721

Additional copies of this book may be ordered from the American Quilter's Society, PO Box 3290, Paducah, KY 42002-3290 @ $24.95. Add $2.00 for postage and handling.

Dedication

*The whole of this book I dedicate
to my husband, Frank,
who has always cared for me and taken care of me.*

AURORA, 86" x 86", made by the author and quilted by Vi Russell. This scrap quilt
is shaded from dark values at the outside edges to light values in the center, using
Sawtooth Stars and Crusader's Cross blocks, with Nine-Patch border stars.

Acknowledgments

Thank you Vi Russell of Quilt Virus in Billings, Montana, Patty Haas of Quilter's Edge, and Edna Gregory of the Silver Thimble in Havre, Montana.

Thanks are extended to computer experts Pete Denniston, Greg Cheever, and Todd Landstad for their computer skills, and to Susan, Jill, and Laura for their unflagging encouragement and support.

Appreciation and admiration go to the quiltmakers who translated sketches into quilts, who took on the challenge of time and distance to produce their personal interpretations of the directions they received, and who, in the process, again proved there is something very special about the people of the HiLine of Montana. Thank you Beaver Aspevig, Diane Jenks, Don Wattam, Edna Gregory, Ethel Siemens, Iona McEwen Schafer, Laura Landstad, Leila King, Lolly Rathbone, Marjorie Chinadle, Mary Ann Wattam, Pat Feeney, Pat Meldrum, Sharon Goodrich, Shirley Anderson, Susan Denniston, Terri Earl, and Lynn Ward.

Preface

There are hexagon stars, octagon stars, and stars in circles. There are four-patch stars, nine-patch stars, and many more. And now there is *Sew Many Stars* with machine techniques for sewing each type of star, step-by-step quilt patterns for beginning to advanced quiltmakers, and useful information for quilters who design with stars – all collected in one source book.

This handbook contains the basic techniques that are simplified and accurate for rotary cutting and machine piecing stars. These methods can be used for other designs as well. This collection provides three methods for piecing the Sawtooth Star, speed techniques for making traditional blocks such as Snowball and Square-Within-a-Square, the never-fail-hassle-free-machine-pieced-eight-pointed-star technique, the perfect miter, and more.

Each technique presented is followed by a quilt pattern incorporating one or more of the methods described. All quilts were designed by the author and interpreted by the quilters with their individual fabric choices. Each technique is represented by a symbol, so you can tell at a glance which ones you will be using for the quilt pattern you have chosen.

This source book is dedicated to those "all-star" quilters who never have enough time to piece all the quilts in their imaginations. These collected classic and new piecing methods are for you.

Contents

BLEST BE THE TIE THAT BINDS, 74" x 74", made by the author.

GREAT NORTHERN STAR , 63" x 71", made by Lynn Ward. Twenty-two rows of stars and bands sewn with paper-backed Seminole piecing meet in the center with Hexagon Stars.

Chapter 1

Half-Squares

The half-square technique is a classic speed-piecing method that produces squares with a diagonal division separating two different fabrics.

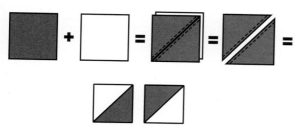

Fig. 1–1. Two at a time

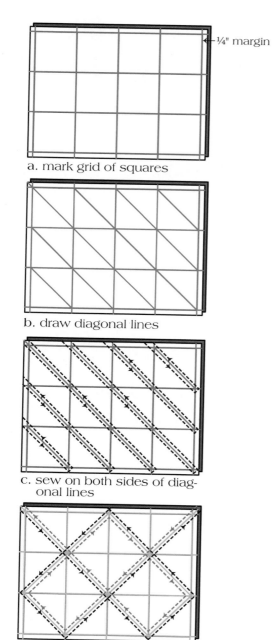

a. mark grid of squares

b. draw diagonal lines

c. sew on both sides of diagonal lines

d. sew to the left of diagonals

Fig. 1–2. Mutliple squares method 1

Two at a time

You can make two half-squares at a time by using the following method (Fig. 1–1):

★ Cut two fabric squares for the half-square ⅞" larger than the required finished square. All seam allowances are included by making the squares ⅞" larger.

★ Place the two fabric squares together with right sides facing.

★ Mark a diagonal line on the wrong side of the top squares.

★ Sew ¼" on both sides of the marked diagonal line.

★ Cut on the marked diagonal line between the two sewn lines.

★ Press open the two triangles created. The result is two matching squares with a diagonal division of fabrics.

Multiple squares

Half-squares can be made by applying the technique for one square to several squares, by marking a grid (Fig. 1–2).

★ Place two fabric pieces, right sides together. Use the cut size, the finished square plus seam allowance, given in the pattern, to mark a grid of squares on the back of the lighter fabric (a). Allow at least ¼" margin around the edges of the grid to keep the outer squares true.

★ Draw diagonal lines through every row of squares (b).

★ Starting in a corner, sew a continuous seam ¼" to the left of all the drawn lines from one edge of the grid to the opposite side. Sew a return seam on the right side of the diagonals (c).

Bias-strip method 1

The bias-strip technique provides a distortion-free means of arriving at the half-square (bias-square). With this technique, bias strips are sewn together and pressed open before the squares are cut. (Fig. 1–4)

★ Cut bias strips the width of the unfinished square.

★ Sew bias strips together lengthwise with a ¼" seam allowance.

★ Press the strips, being careful not to stretch the bias edges.

★ Make a template the size of the half-square plus seam allowances.

★ Place the template on the strips on point, aligning the top and bottom corners with the seam line.

★ Cut around the template to make the half-squares.

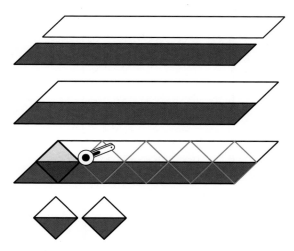

Fig. 1–4. Bias-strip method 1

Bias-strip method 2

Make several half-squares at a time from fabric squares or rectangles (Fig. 1–5).

★ Place two squares right sides together with the lightest one on top.

★ Draw diagonal (45°) lines the required width, stated in your pattern, across the top fat quarter.

★ Sew ¼" on both sides of each line. Cut the strips apart on the lines.

★ Use a template to cut triangles in zigzag fashion along both edges to complete the half-squares.

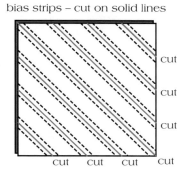

bias strips – cut on solid lines

cut
cut
cut
cut   cut   cut   cut

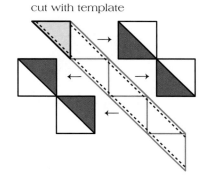

cut with template

Fig. 1–5. Bias-strip method 2

Measurements for cutting half-squares

To find the cut size of the squares, first determine the length of the short sides of the *finished* half-squares. Add ⅞" for seam allowances. *Example:* For two 3" finished half-squares, start with two 3⅞" squares.

For greater accuracy, try adding 1" instead of ⅞" for seam allowances. Then, after sewing and pressing the squares, trim them to the proper measurement.

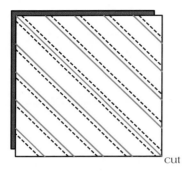

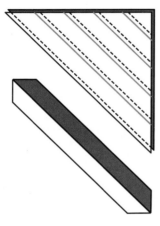

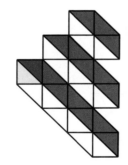

Bias-strip method 3

Here is another method for making multiple half-squares from bias strips Fig. 1–6).

★ Place two fat quarters, right sides together. Draw 45° lines the required width across the top fat quarter.

★ Stitch ¼" on both sides of the center line and stitch ¼" on only one side of the remaining lines, as shown in Fig. 1–6. This method yields the longest possible strips.

★ Cut the pairs of strips apart and sew the pairs together for the most efficient use of fabric. Use a template to cut the half-squares.

Fig. 1–6. Bias-strip method 3

Measurements for cutting bias-squares

✰ ✰ ✰

The width of the strips needed to make bias-squares is equal to the cut size of the square. *Example:* For a square that finishes 2", the cut size of the bias strips is 2½".

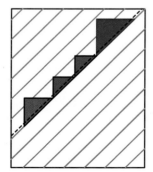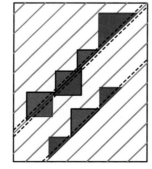

Fig. 1–7 Save scrap triangles

Corner triangles in diagonal sets

✰ ✰ ✰

The ⅞" half-square formula also applies to triangles used for the corners of diagonally set quilts. To find the size of the squares needed to make the corner triangles, use the finished size of the quilt blocks and add ⅞". *Example:* For a quilt made of 12" (finished size) Variable Star blocks on point, add ⅞" to 12". Therefore, you will need two 12⅞" squares cut in half diagonally to make the four corner setting triangles.

Save scrap triangles

The bias-strip technique can be adapted for saving scrap triangles. Use the following technique to save both time and fabric (Fig. 1–7):

★ First, determine the smallest square you are willing to sew; 1½" cut squares that will finish as 1" half-squares.

★ Select a background color, draw parallel diagonal lines 1½" apart on the right side of the background fabric.

★ Sew waste triangles tip to tip, along the drawn lines, using a ¼" seam allowance.

★ When the background fabric has been covered with scrap triangles, cut the parallel strips apart on the drawn lines. Press open the triangles. Trim the half-squares to the 1½" size for future projects.

ADVANTAGES AND DISADVANTAGES

The grid and strip techniques are fast and easy if you need more than a handful of half-squares. The choice of whether to use a straight-grain (Fig.1–8) or a bias technique (Fig.1–9) can be determined by the amount of fabric available. For example, more half-squares can be cut from two fat quarters by using the straight-grain techniques rather than the bias ones, as the bias cuts produce more "waste" scraps.

A disadvantage of the straight-grain techniques is that the half-squares can be distorted when they are pressed. To solve this problem, start with oversized squares and then trim them to size after they have been sewn and pressed.

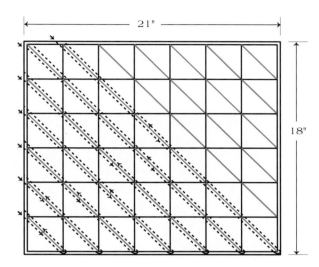

make 2" finished half-squares from two fat quarters
2⅞" grid = 84 half-squares

Fig. 1–8. Straight-grain technique

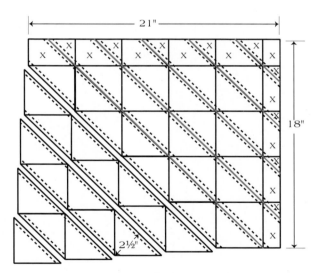

2½" bias strips = 40 half-squares
X = waste

Fig. 1–9. Bias technique

Save leftover binding

✧ ✧ ✧

Use the bias-strip method to make leftover bias-binding strips into half-squares. The resulting half-squares are more convenient to store and use than the binding strips.

HUNTER'S STAR, 32" x 32", made by the author.

HUNTER'S STAR
32" x 32"

16 Hunter's Star units, 5"

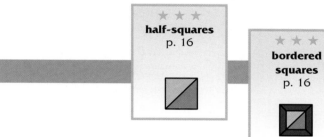

★ ★ ★
half-squares
p. 16

★ ★ ★
bordered squares
p. 16

Cut strips selvage to selvage. Be sure to label all your pieces with their cut sizes.
If you prefer, you can use scraps for the light and medium blue squares.

Materials	Yds.	First cut		Second cut	
Lt. blue	½	1 strip	3⅞"	8 squares	3⅞"
		2 strip	4"	16 squares	4"
Med. blue	½	1 strip	3⅞"	8 squares	3⅞"
		2 strip	4"	16 squares	4"
Dk. blue stars	⅝	11 strips	1½"	64 rectangles	1½" x 6¼"
Borders					
Dk. blue	½	4 strips	3⅝"		
Brown	⅜	4 strips	2¾"		
Accent	¼	4 strips	1"		
Backing	1	1 panel	36" x 36"		
Binding	½				
Batting		36" x 36"			

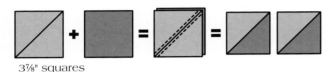

3⅞" squares

Fig. 1–9. Half-squares

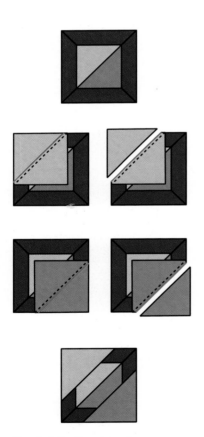

Fig. 1–10. Bordered squares

Sewing

The directions for the Hunter's Star wall-hanging that follow describe the uses of the half-square and a bordered-square technique to sew the blocks.

BLOCK ASSEMBLY

Half-squares

★ Place a 3⅞" medium blue square and a 3⅞" light blue square right sides together. Draw a diagonal line from corner to corner on the top one.

★ Sew ¼" on both sides of the line. Cut the squares apart on the drawn line to make two half-squares. Repeat to make a total of 16 half-squares (Fig. 1–9).

Bordered squares

★ To make the dark blue star points, border the 16 half-squares with the 1½" x 6¼" dark blue strips. Cut 45° angles at each end of the border strips, as shown (Fig. 1–10). Miter the corners.

★ Place a 4" light blue square, right sides together, in the corner of the matching light blue half of a bordered half-square. Place a 4" medium blue square in the corner of the matching medium blue half.

★ Draw a diagonal line on the backs of the 4" squares, parallel to the half-square seam line. Sew on the drawn lines. Allow a ¼" seam allowance and cut away the waste triangles. Complete all 16 blocks in this manner.

QUILT ASSEMBLY

It takes four 5" blocks to create a star. Sew four blocks across and four blocks down for the wallhanging.

★ Sew the three border strips together, as shown in the Quilt Assembly diagram (Fig. 1–11). Sew the combined border widths to each side of the wallhanging and miter the corners.

FINISHING

Layer the quilt with the batting and backing and quilt as desired. The wall quilt in the photo was hand quilted ¼" inside the seams in the center with a machine quilted border design. Bind the raw edges of the quilt with 2" continuous, double-fold bias binding.

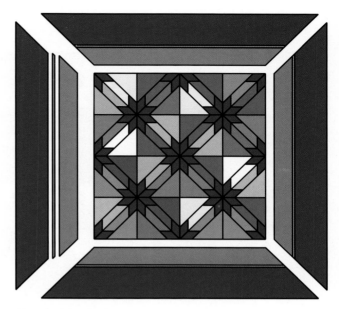

Fig. 1–11. Quilt assembly

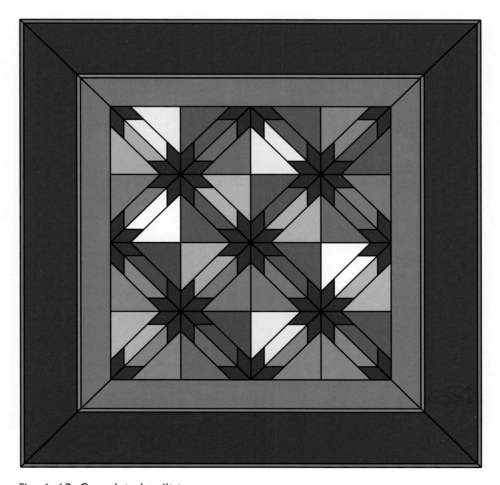

Fig. 1–12. Completed quilt top

HUNTER'S STAR, 80" x 97", made by Terri Earl. Use the Half-square and Bordered-square techniques on page 16 to make the Hunter's Star blocks for this bed-size quilt.

SEW MANY STARS – *Gail Searl*

Chapter 2

Double Half-Squares

The double half-square is a rectangle with a diagonal stripe that is created by top and bottom triangles.

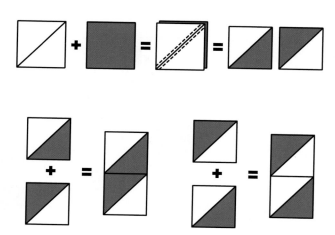

Fig. 2–1. Two half-squares

The double half-square can be made in several different ways. The following five methods do not require templates for cutting.

Two half-squares

Double half-squares can be made by sewing two half-squares together (Fig. 2–1).

★ Sew a light and a dark square together to make two half-squares.

★ Sew the light halves of the squares together to create a light diagonal stripe. Sew the dark halves together for a dark diagonal stripe.

Measurements for cutting half-square methods

To find the cut size of the squares needed to make the half-squares, add ⅞" to the width of the finished double half-square. *Example:* To sew a 2" x 4" (finished) double half-square, cut one 2⅞" dark square and one 2⅞" light square.

Corner-squares

To make double half-squares without a seam in the diagonal stripe, use the corner-square technique (Fig. 2–2).

★ Place a square on one end of a rectangle, right sides together.

★ Draw a diagonal line across the square, corner to corner, and sew on the drawn line.

★ Sew another square to the other end of the rectangle, making sure that the sewing lines are parallel to each other. (To make mirror-image rectangles, stitch both squares of a second rectangle on the opposite diagonal.)

★ Cut off the waste triangles, leaving a ¼" seam allowance. Open the sewn triangles and press.

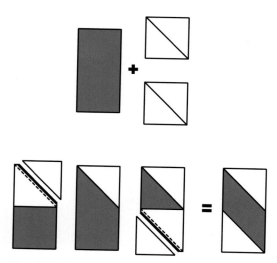

Fig. 2–2. Corner-squares

Measurements for cutting corner-squares

⭐ ⭐ ⭐

Determine the finished size of the double half-square you need. Cut a rectangle the size of the diagonal stripe plus ½" seam allowances. The cut size for the two squares is the width of this rectangle. *Example:* To sew a 2" x 4" finished double half-square, cut one 2½" x 4½" rectangle for the center stripe and two 2½" squares for the corner triangles.

Strip method 1

To create several double half-squares at a time, use strips (Fig. 2–3).

- ★ Cut two strips for making the corner triangles and one wider strip for the diagonal stripe.
- ★ Sew the three strips together lengthwise with the wider one in the middle. Do not press the layered strips open, yet. The two outside strips will overlap each other in the center.
- ★ Use a rotary cutter and ruler to cut slices from the layered strips, producing rectangles with squares attached.
- ★ Draw parallel diagonal lines on both of the squares. Slant the diagonals either to the right or to the left, according to the requirements of the block.
- ★ Fold one of the squares out of the way and sew on the drawn diagonal line of the other square. Repeat for the second square.
- ★ Cut off the waste triangles. Pick out the stitches at the corners to allow the squares to be pressed open.

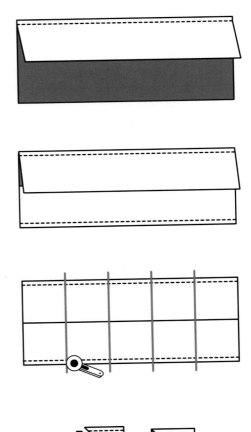

Fig. 2–3. Strip method 1

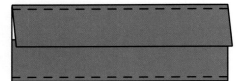

a. baste narrow strips to wide strip

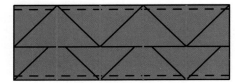

b. draw diagonal lines on outer strips

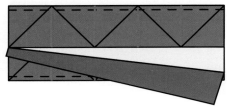

c. move bottom strip out of the way

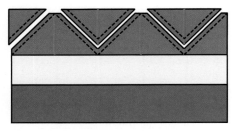

d. remove waste triangles

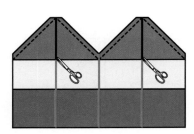

e. cut top fabric only

Fig. 2–4. Strip method 2

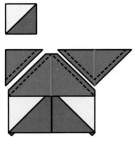

f. cut the half-squares apart and set aside

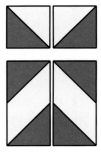

method yields mirror-image double half-squares and corner squares

Strip method 2

To make multiple corner squares, sew strips of fabric in a zigzag line to create mirror-image double half-squares (Fig. 2–4).

★ Cut two narrow strips for making the corner triangles and one wider strip for the diagonal stripe.

★ Baste one narrow strip on each side of the wider strip. The two outer strips will overlap in the center (a).

★ Use the same measurement as the cut width of the narrow strip to mark lines across the basted strips.

★ Draw diagonal lines across the squares, corner to corner, making a zigzag sewing line (b). Sew on the zigzag line on the top strip (c).

★ Cut the top strip only on the drawn line from the base to the tip of each triangle (d). Press the corner triangles open.

★ Repeat the steps to sew and cut the bottom strip. Cut the double half-squares apart and press the corner triangles open.

★ Optional: Stitch a second seam a scant seam allowance above the first stitching line (d). Remove the basting stitches from the top strip. Cut between the stitching lines to remove the extra triangles (e). Cut the triangles on the line to make half-squares to set aside for another project (f).

Measurements for cutting strip methods 1 & 2

★ ★ ★

Determine the finished size of the double half-square needed. Cut a rectangle the size of the finished rectangle plus ½" seam allowances. The cut size for the two squares is the width of this rectangle. *Example*: For a 2" x 4" finished double half-square, cut the center strip 4½" and the other two strips 2½" wide. Cut 2½" slices across the strips.

The advantage of the corner-square strip method for making double half-squares is that all the squares are correctly positioned on the rectangles, which cuts down the handling time involved.

Bias strips

Double half-squares can be made by sewing triangles to bias-cut strips. This technique requires precise cutting, sewing, and pressing. You may want to practice this technique with scraps before cutting the fabrics for your quilt (Fig. 2–5).

★ Stabilize the fabric for the bias strips by ironing with sizing. Cut bias strips the width given in the pattern (a).

★ Staystitch both edges of the bias strips within the ¼" seam allowances (b).

★ From a different fabric, cut several half-square triangles (c).

★ Place triangles face down on one edge of the bias strip. The tips of the triangles should be touching (d).

★ Stitch the triangles to the bias strip with a ¼" seam allowance. Press the triangles away from the strip.

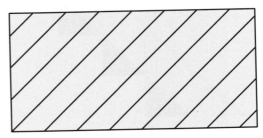

a. cut bias strips

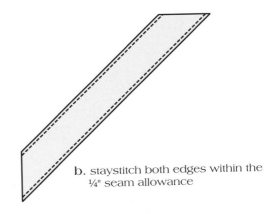

b. staystitch both edges within the ¼" seam allowance

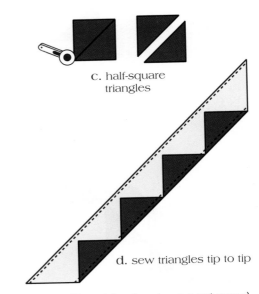

c. half-square triangles

d. sew triangles tip to tip

Fig. 2–5. Bias strips (cont. on next page)

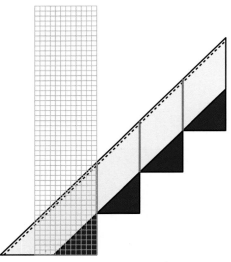

e. draw lines, place triangles
into angles of drawn lines

★ Place a ruler even with the bottom and side of each triangle (e). Draw across the bias strip. (To make double half-squares in mirror image, draw the lines as shown in f.)

★ On the opposite side of the bias strip, tuck triangles into the angles created by the drawn lines (g) and sew them to the strip. Press the triangles away from the strip (h).

★ Cut the double half-squares from the strip (h).

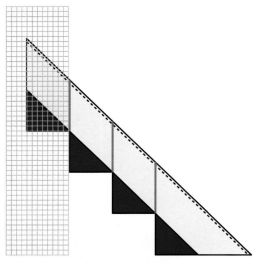

f. mirror image

Measurements for bias-strip methods

☆ ☆ ☆

First draw the finished rectangle to find the strip width needed for the diagonal stripe. Measure the width of the stripe needed and add ½" for seam allowances. Measure the short side of one of the triangles and add ⅞" to determine the width of the squares to be cut for triangles. *Example:* For a rectangle that finishes 2" x 4", the width of the bias strip for the diagonal stripe will be 1¹⁵⁄₁₆", including seam allowances. The squares for the triangles will be 2⅞".

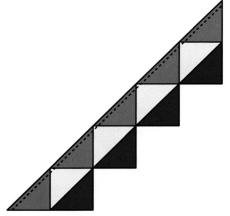

g. press triangles open
   sew second row of
   triangles

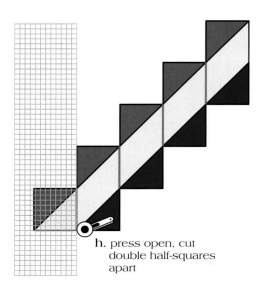

h. press open, cut
   double half-squares
   apart

Fig. 2–5. Bias-strips, continued

PRAIRIE HOME, 32" x 32", made by Don Wattam and Mary Ann Wattam. The pattern for a bed-size quilt with a different coloration of the Indian Meadow block begins on page 27.

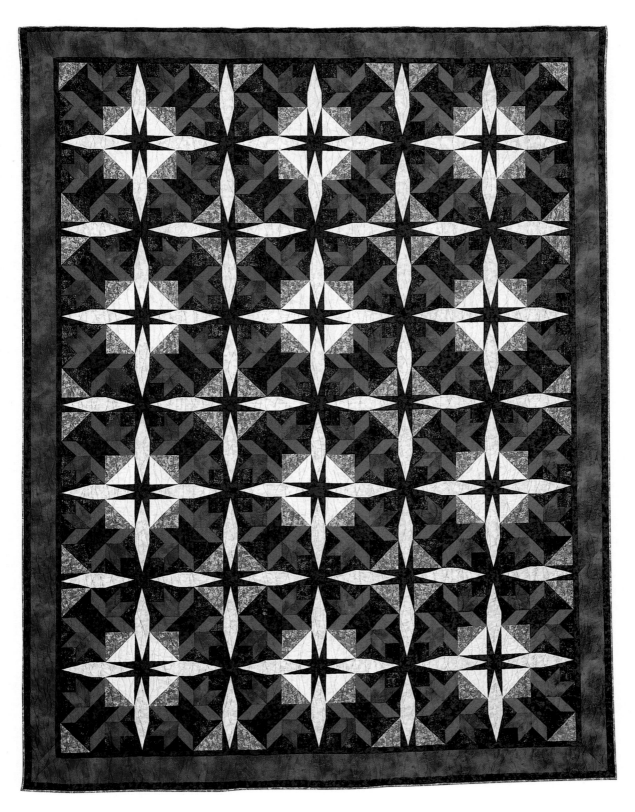

PRAIRIE HOMESTEAD, 80½" x 104½", designed and pieced by the
author and quilted by Vi Russell.

PRAIRIE HOMESTEAD

80½" x 104½"

48 Indian Meadow Blocks, 10" 
82 Lattice Strips, 2" x 10"

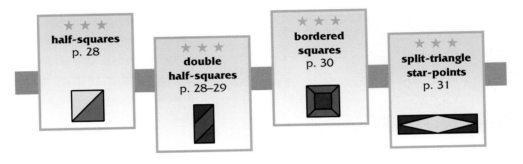

★ ★ ★
half-squares
p. 28

★ ★ ★
**double
half-squares**
p. 28–29

★ ★ ★
**bordered
squares**
p. 30

★ ★ ★
**split-triangle
star-points**
p. 31

Cut strips selvage to selvage. Be sure to label all your pieces with their cut sizes.

Materials	Yds.	First cut		Second cut	
Purple	4⅜	6 strips	2½"	83 squares	2½"
		13 strips	6⅛"		
		7 strips	2⅞"	96 squares	2⅞"
BORDER 1		9 strips	1¼"		
BORDER 3		10 strips	1½"		
Pale Yellow	⅝	3 strips	5"	24 squares	5"
Lt. Brown	2¼	6 strips	10½"	82 rectangles	2½" x 10½"
Med. Brown	1¾	6 strips	5"	48 squares	5"
BINDING		1 square	28"		
Dk. Brown	2⅞	3 strips	5"	24 squares	5"
		7 strips	2⅞"	96 squares	2⅞"
		4 strips	5½"	24 squares	5½"
		12 strips	2½"	192 squares	2½ "
Red 1	3	6 strips	10¼"	96 rectangles	2½" x 10¼"
BORDER 2		10 strips	4"		
Red 2	2⅛	7 rectangles	18" x 21"	bias strips	2"
Backing	7½	3 panels	37" x 84½"		
Batting		84½" x 108½"			

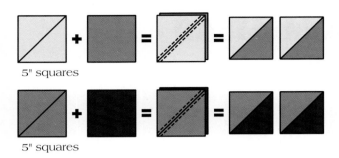

5" squares

5" squares

Fig. 2–6. Half-squares

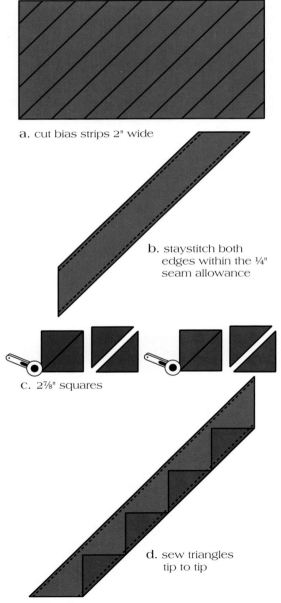

a. cut bias strips 2" wide

b. staystitch both
edges within the ¼"
seam allowance

c. 2⅞" squares

d. sew triangles
tip to tip

Fig. 2–7. Double half-squares

Sewing

The PRAIRIE HOMESTEAD quilt uses the traditional half-square technique and the double half-square technique. The sashing is made with split triangles.

BLOCK ASSEMBLY

Half-squares: Sew two half-squares for each of the 48 Indian Meadow blocks by using the following traditional half-square technique:

★ Place a 5" pale yellow square on a 5" medium brown square, right sides together. Draw a diagonal line, corner to corner, on the top square. Sew ¼" seams on both sides of the drawn line. Cut the square in half diagonally. Press open. Trim the square to measure 4½".

★ Make 24 pale yellow/medium brown half-squares and 24 medium-brown/dark-brown half-squares. Press. Trim the squares to measure 4½" (Fig. 2–6).

Double half-squares: Each of the Indian Meadow blocks contains four double half-squares 2½" x 4½", unfinished (Fig. 2–7). Note that two of the rectangles are mirror images.

★ Stabilize the red-2 fabric by ironing it with commercial spray sizing. Cut 2"-wide bias strips across the fabric (a). Staystitch both edges of the bias strips (b). Trim the strips to 1¹⁵⁄₁₆". (If ruler measures only eighths, center the edge of strip between 1⅞" and 2" by eye.)

★ Cut the 2⅞" purple and the 2⅞" dark brown squares in half diagonally to make 192 half-square triangles of each color (c).

★ Sew 96 dark brown triangles, tip to tip and face down on the bias strips, aligning the long edges of the triangles with the right edges of the strips (d). Press the triangles away from the bias strips.

★ Place a ruler even with the bottom and right side of each triangle. Draw a line across the bias strip (e).

★ Position the purple triangles on the opposite sides of the bias strips so the triangles are tucked into the angles created by the drawn lines. Sew the purple triangles to the bias strips (f). Press the triangles away from the strips (g).

★ Cut the double half-squares away from the bias strip by cutting on the drawn lines. Measure 2½" from one edge to trim each piece (h). Make 96 double half-squares.

★ To make 96 mirror-image double half-squares, use the same technique but draw the lines across the bias strips in the other direction (i).

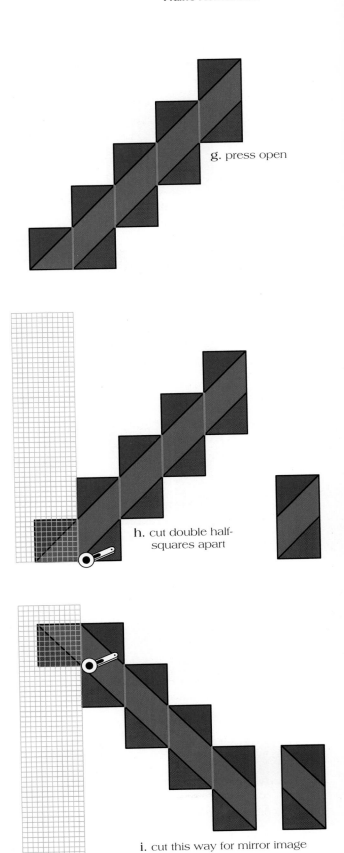

g. press open

h. cut double half-squares apart

i. cut this way for mirror image

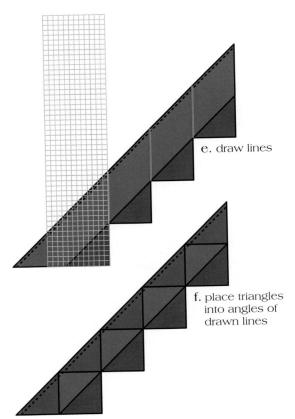

e. draw lines

f. place triangles into angles of drawn lines

Fig. 2–7. Double half-squares, continued

a. cut using 2½" x 10¼" template

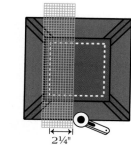

b. stitch the miters

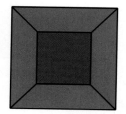

2¼"

c. cut 2¼" from seam line

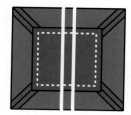

d. rotate the square and cut again

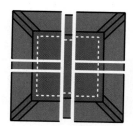

e. cut the halves into quarters

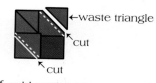
←waste triangle
cut
cut

f. add corner squares

g. finished unit

Fig. 2–8. Bordered squares

Bordered squares: The red-1 star points are presewn to the dark brown squares in the corners of the blocks. The star-point units are cut from bordered squares, as follows:

★ To make a template for the borders, cut a 2½" x 10¼" paper rectangle. Fold the upper-left and the upper-right corners down to meet the lower edge of the rectangle, making a wedge shape. Paste the wedge to template plastic and cut out the template.

★ Use the template to alternate the cutting of the wedge shapes from edge to edge along the 2½" red-1 strips (a).

★ Sew a red-1 border to each side of the 24 5½" dark brown squares. Miter the corners (b).

★ Turn the two border squares to the wrong side. Cut the bordered square into quarters, as follows: Place the 2¼" line of the ruler on the seam line that joins the border to the square (c). Slice across the square.

★ Rotate the block and cut the other half of the bordered square in the same way (d). Cut the block two more times to make quarters (e). Discard the scraps. Cut all 24 dark brown bordered squares into quarters.

★ Place 2½" dark brown squares on the two corners on either side of the miters for each quarter. Sew diagonally and parallel to the miter across the squares, corner to corner (f).

★ Cut away the waste triangles, leaving a ¼" seam allowance to complete the star-point units (g).

Split-triangle star points: The lattice pieces have two purple star points at each end and can be made with the split-triangle technique as follows:

★ Spray the wrong sides of the 6⅛" purple strips with sizing and press them. Be careful not to distort them as you press.

★ On the wrong sides of the pieces, draw vertical lines every 1½" along the length of the strips (a).

★ Cut triangles across the strips as shown in a. Note that each V has a vertical line through the center.

★ Fold each 2½" x 10½" light brown sashing rectangle in half. Finger press a crease to mark the midpoint of the rectangle (b).

★ Place a purple triangle right side down, with the tip at the midpoint of the rectangle, and align the side of the triangle with the side of the rectangle, as shown in (c).

★ Sew the triangle to the lattice rectangle on the drawn line. Apply a second triangle on the same side of the rectangle at the opposite end (d). Turn the piece to the wrong side. Trim the triangles even with the sashing rectangle. *Optional:* Trim the extra fabric off both triangles, leaving ¼" seam allowance. (e). Press open.

★ Sew two more triangles to the opposite side of the sashing rectangle (f).

★ Handle the sashing strips with care because the star points are not on the straight of grain. Make 82 lattice units.

QUILT ASSEMBLY

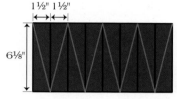

a. cutting lines shown in red

b. fold in half and crease

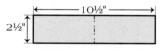

c. align the triangle point with the crease

d. sew on drawn line

e. trim leaving ¼" seam allowances

f. finished lattice unit

Fig. 2–9. Split-triangle star points

a. combine blocks and lattice
units into four-block units

Sew the quilt into units of four blocks with yellow/brown half-square triangles surrounding a lattice strip "cross" that has a purple 2½" square at the center (a). Make 12 four-block units (b).

★ Make 17 lattice strips consisting of two lattice units with a purple 2½" square in the middle (c).

★ Sew three large blocks and two lattice strips together, as shown, to make a block row (d). Make four block rows.

★ Sew three lattice strips, end to end, to make a lattice row. Make three lattice rows (e). Sew all the rows together.

FINISHING

Stitch the borders to the quilt edges and miter the corners. Layer the quilt with batting and backing, then quilt the layers. Bind the raw edges of the quilt with 2" continuous, double-fold bias binding (Fig. 2–11).

b. finished four-block unit

c. lattice strip

d. block row

e. lattice row

Fig. 2–10. Quilt assembly

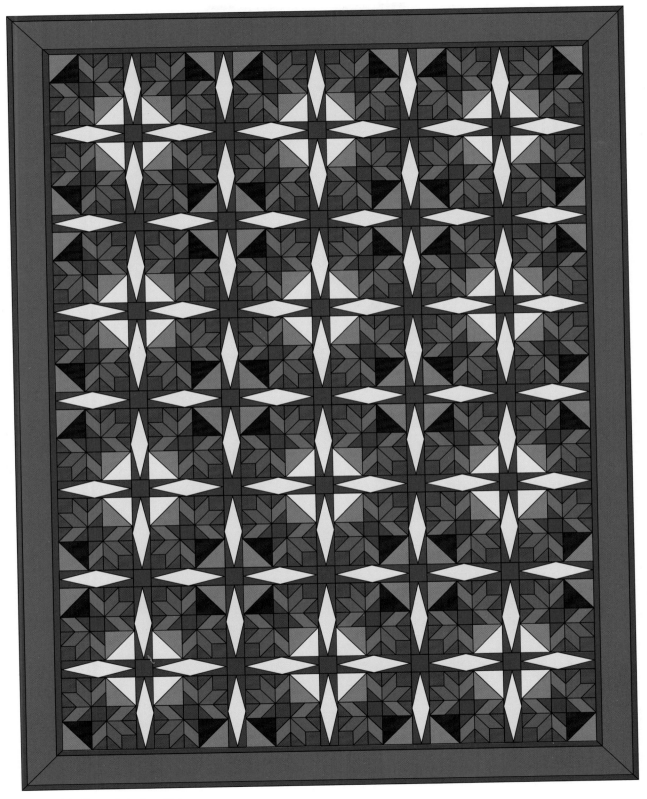

Fig. 2–11. Completed quilt top

POINSETTIA, 24" x 40", made by Ethel Siemens.

POINSETTIA
24" x 40"

3 Clay's Choice Blocks, 8"

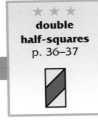

★ ★ ★
**double
half-squares**
p. 36–37

★ ★ ★
**quarter-square
triangle units**
p. 38

Cut strips selvage to selvage. Be sure to label all your pieces with their cut sizes.

Materials	Yds.	First cut		Second cut	
Red	¾	1 strip	18"	1 square 15"	
BINDING				1 square 18"	
RIBBON BOW		1 strip	2½"		
Red print	1	1 rectangle	18" X 21"		
		2 strips	2½"		
		2 strips	1¹⁵⁄₁₆" star points		
RIBBON BOW		1 strip	2½"		
Med. Green	⅜	1 strip	3¼" layered cutting		
		2 strips	1¹⁵⁄₁₆" strip piecing		
Dk. Green	⅛	1 strip	3¼" layered cutting		
White	1⅛	1 strip	2½"	12 squares	2½"
		5 strips	2⅞"	66 squares	2⅞"
		1 strip	5¼"	2 squares	5¼"
BORDER		8 strips	1½"		
Backing	1¼	1 panel	28" X 44"		
Batting		28" X 44"			

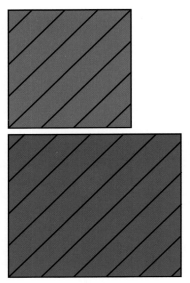

a. cut bias strips 2" wide

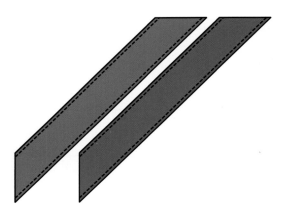

b. trim to 1¹⁵⁄₁₆"; staystitch both edges
within the ¼" seam allowance

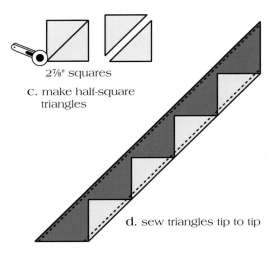

2⅞" squares

c. make half-square
triangles

d. sew triangles tip to tip

Fig. 2–12. Double half-squares

Sewing

The Poinsettia wallhanging contains three Clay's Choice blocks surrounded by half stars. Unlike most other star patterns in this book, the star points are pieced to the corner squares rather than the base triangles.

The 6" x 12" rotary ruler and the 6" x 6" bias square are recommended for this project. The double half-square rectangle directions that follow require accurate cutting and piecing. Test the accuracy of your sewing of these units before proceeding with all of them. Fabric allowances are adequate for half-square and corner-square techniques.

Block Assembly

Double half-squares: Use the bias-strip method to make the red and white double half-squares used in the blocks and the ribbon border, as follows:

★ Cut 2"-wide red bias strips, as needed, from the 15" red square and the 18" x 21" red print rectangle (a). Staystitch the bias edge (b). Trim the strips to 1¹⁵⁄₁₆" wide. (If your ruler is not marked in sixteenths, place the edge of each strip half way between 1⅞" and 2" by eye.)

★ Cut each 2⅞" white square in half once diagonally to make 132 half-square triangles (c). Use 72 of the triangles for the bias-strip double half-square method. Set the rest aside for the borders.

★ Make 12 red and 12 red-print double half-squares that slant from the lower left to the upper right (Fig. d–h). Make 12 additional red-print double half-squares that slant from the lower right to the upper left (i).

e. draw lines

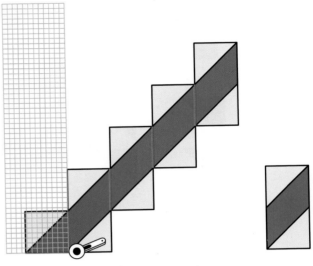

h. cut double half-squares apart

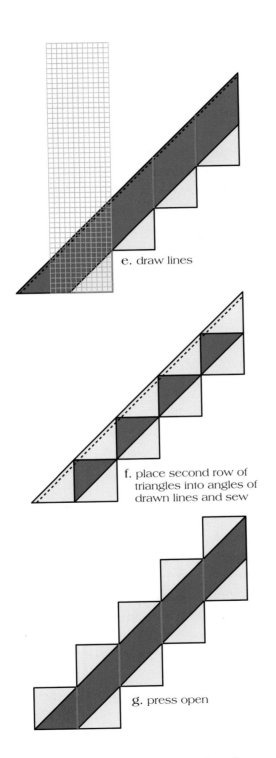

f. place second row of
triangles into angles of
drawn lines and sew

g. press open

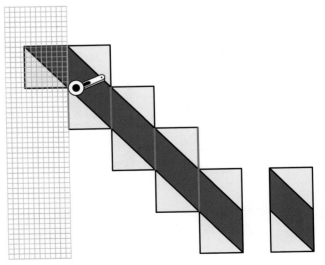

i. cut this way for mirror image

Fig. 2–12. Double half-squares, continued

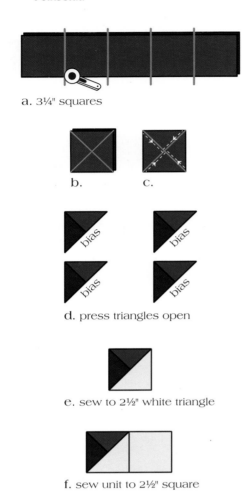

a. 3¼" squares

b.   c.

d. press triangles open

e. sew to 2½" white triangle

f. sew unit to 2½" square

Fig. 2–13. Quarter-square triangle units

Quarter-square triangle units: Place the 3¼"-wide medium green strip on top of the 3¼" dark green strip, right sides together. Cut eight 3¼" squares from the layered strips (Fig 2–13a).

★ Use a fine pencil to draw an X from corner to corner on the back of the medium green squares.

★ Starting at each corner and stopping in the center, sew seams ¼" to the left of the drawn lines (c). Sew all eight pairs of squares in the same manner.

★ Cut the squares apart on the drawn lines and press the identical two-tone green triangles open (d).

★ Sew the 32 two-tone green triangles to 32 of the white triangles (e). Press open. Sew 12 of these units to the 2½" white squares (f).

Finish blocks: Refer to the Block Assembly diagram to finish the blocks (Fig. 2–14). In the center of each block, pick out the stitches in the seam allowances so they can be fanned counter clockwise. Press. Sew three blocks together in a row.

STAR BORDER

Star-point units

★ For the star points, place a 1¹⁵⁄₁₆" green and a 1¹⁵⁄₁₆" red strip right sides together (Fig. 2–15a, page 41). Sew a seam on one long edge. Do not press open.

★ Place the layers green side up. Cutting at a 45° angle through both layers, make 20 slices 2½" wide (b). Press open.

★ Retrieve 20 of the two-color green and white squares. Sew them to the red and green star points with a set-in seam to complete the star-point units (c).

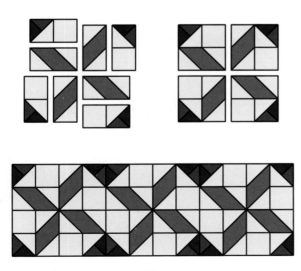

Fig. 2–14. Block assembly

Half- and quarter-star blocks

★ Cut the two 5¼" white squares in half diagonally twice to make eight base triangles (Fig 2–16). Sew two star-point units to each base triangle.

★ Add two 2⅞" white half-square triangles to each unit, as shown, to complete the half-star blocks. Sew two 2⅞" white half-square triangles to the remaining four star-point units to complete the quarter-star blocks for the corners.

★ Sew three star halves together to make a 24½" row (e). Make a second row like this. Sew the star rows to the long sides of the Clay's Choice blocks.

★ Sew a quarter-star block to each end of the remaining two half-star blocks and sew these strips to the top and bottom of the quilt.

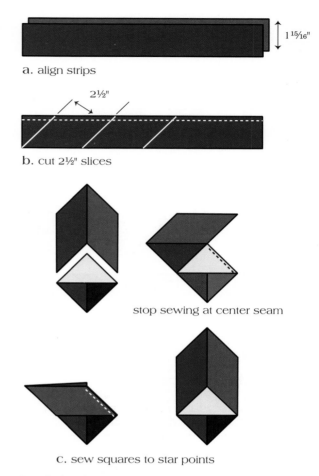

a. align strips

1 15/16"

2½"

b. cut 2½" slices

stop sewing at center seam

c. sew squares to star points

Fig. 2–15. Star-point units

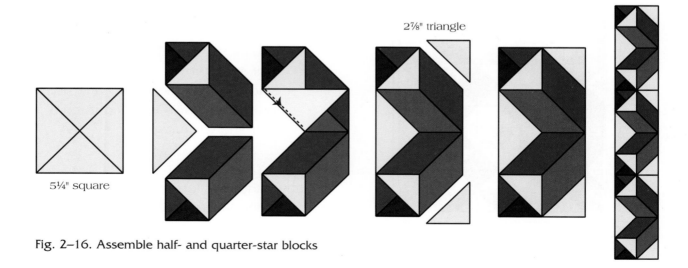

2⅞" triangle

5¼" square

Fig. 2–16. Assemble half- and quarter-star blocks

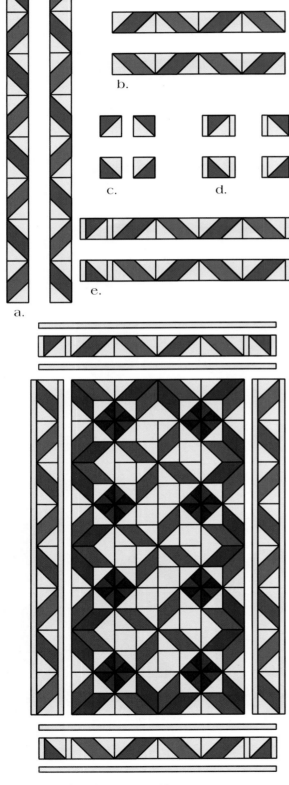

Fig. 2–17. Quilt assembly

REMAINING BORDERS

★ From the 1½" white border strips, cut four borders 24½" long, four borders 32½" long, and eight rectangles 2½" long.

★ For the ribbon border, sew eight print and plain double half-squares, end to end, for the right side of the quilt and eight for the left (Fig. 2–17a).

★ Sew a ½" x 32" white strip to both sides of the two ribbon borders, and sew these border units to the sides of the quilt (see quilt assembly).

★ For the top ribbon border, sew four double half-squares, end to end. Sew four for the bottom (b).

★ Use the leftovers from making the red-print and white bias double half-squares to make four 2½" half-squares for the corners (c).

★ Position the half-squares so that the red half points outward from each of the four corners of the quilt.

★ Sew a 1½" x 2½" white rectangle to two sides of the four half squares as shown in (d).

★ Sew the half-square units to each end of the top and bottom ribbon borders (e).

★ Enclose the top and bottom borders with the 1½" x 24½" white strips (see quilt assembly).

★ Stitch the completed top and bottom ribbon rows in place to complete the wallhanging.

FINISHING

Layer the quilt top with batting and backing. Quilt the layers as desired. Poinsettia is quilted all over with a meandering line. Sew continuous 2" double-fold bias binding from the 18" red square. Randomly stitch gold beads to embellish the quilt.

Fig. 2–18. Completed quilt top. For the ribbon detail, use 2½" x 42" strips of red and red print fabrics. Sew all four sides leaving a 4" opening for turning. Tie bow and tack to quilt as shown in photograph on page 34.

SEW MANY STARS - *Gail Searl*

FAR EAST, 80" x 92", pieced by the author and quilted by Vi Russell.
Variable Star blocks are made using quarter-squares, page 44.

Chapter 3

Quarter-Squares

The quarter-square is a square divided diagonally twice. The four divisions of the square are triangles.

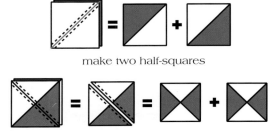

make two half-squares

use half-squares to make quarter-squares

Fig. 3–1. Half-square method

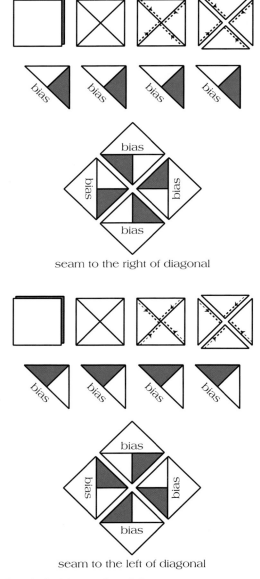

seam to the right of diagonal

seam to the left of diagonal

Fig. 3–2. Identical eighths

Quarter-squares from half-squares

Two quarter-squares can be made from two half-squares (Fig. 3–1).

★ Place two half-squares, right sides together, with colors not matching.

★ On the wrong side of the top half-square, draw a line corner to corner on the diagonal opposite the seam line.

★ Sew ¼" seams on both sides of the drawn line.

★ Cut on the drawn line and press the two resulting quarter-squares.

Please note that some quilters find it more accurate to cut the half-squares diagonally in half before sewing the resulting triangles into quarter-squares.

Identical Eighths

Sew from each corner of a square; stop at the square's center. Sew only on one side of the square's diagonal to produce identical eighths. Cut the squares diagonally in quarters to yield two triangles that are identical eighths (Fig. 3–2).

★ Draw both diagonals, from corner to corner, on the top square.

★ Place light square on top of the dark square.

★ Sew from one corner to the center. Stop in the middle at the intersecting drawn line. Repeat for each corner.

★ Sew consistently either to the right of the drawn lines or to the left to determine the positions of the colors.

★ Cut on both diagonal lines and press the 2 pairs of triangles. These can be sewn together to make two quarter-square blocks.

Grid method for identical eighths

Several pairs of quarter-square triangles can be made at the same time by using the grid method. Fabric fat quarters (approximately 18" x 21") are a convenient size for this technique (Fig. 3–3).

★ Place two fat quarters, with the lighter one on top and right sides together. Using the cut size given in the pattern, mark a grid of squares on the wrong side of the top fabric. Allow at least ¼" margin around the edges of the fat quarters to keep the outer squares true.

★ Draw lines through both diagonals in all the squares, so that each square has an "X" in it.

★ At one corner of a square, begin sewing on the left side of a drawn line, with a ¼" seam allowance. At the center of each "X", jog to the right side of the line. Return to stitching on the left side at the beginning of the next square and jog to the right at the center. Continue sewing each square in this manner.

★ In a like manner, sew the opposite diagonals. Separate the pairs of triangles by cutting on all the drawn lines. Each square in the grid will produce four identical two-color quarter-square triangles. The darker triangle will be on the left.

Note: To have the darker triangle on the right, place the lighter square on top. Sew on the right side of the diagonal and jog to left at the center of each square.

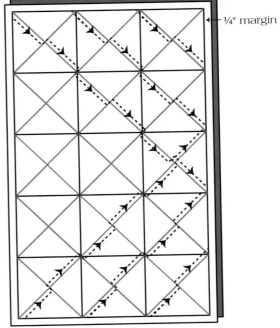

¼" margin

continue sewing as shown; repeat for the opposite diagonals

Fig. 3–3. Grid method for identical eighths

Measurements for cutting quarter-squares

☆ ☆ ☆

To find the size of the cut square needed to make quarter-squares, first determine the length of the side of the finished square. Add 1¼" for seam allowances. *Example:* For 3" finished quarter-squares, cut the squares 4¼".

STARS, SPOOLS, AND CHECKS, 48" x 48", pieced by Lolly Rathbone
and quilted by Vi Russell.

STARS, SPOOLS, AND CHECKS
48" x 48"

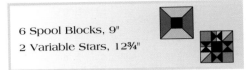

6 Spool Blocks, 9"

2 Variable Stars, 12¾"

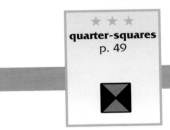

quarter-squares
p. 49

half-squares
p. 49

**tri-color
quarter-squares**
p. 49

Cut strips selvage to selvage. Be sure to label all your pieces with their cut sizes.

Materials	Yds.	First cut	Second cut
Black	⅞	5 strips	3½"
		4 strips	2"
Black print	⅜	6 squares	3½"
		2 squares	4¾"
		4 squares	5½"
Green print	¾	3 strips	3½"
		3 squares	10¼"
		1 square	7¼"
Red	¾	1 strip	3½"
		1 strip	2"
		2 squares	10¼"
		1 square	7¼"
		2 squares	4¾"
		1 square	5½"
		2 rectangles	3" x 5½"
		1 square	5⅛"
Red print	⅜	2 strips	3½"
		1 strip	2"
Gold	1	5 strips	3½"
		2 strips	2"
		2 squares	10¼"
		2 squares	5½"
		2 rectangles	3" x 5½"
		1 square	5⅛"
		4 squares	4¾"
Backing	3	2 panels	26½" x 52"
Binding	⅝		
Batting		52" x 52"	

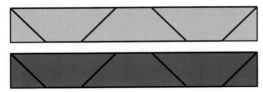

a. cut using 3½" x 10¼" template

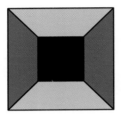

b. border black print with wedges

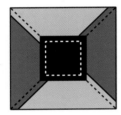

c. press allowances

Fig. 3–4. Spool blocks

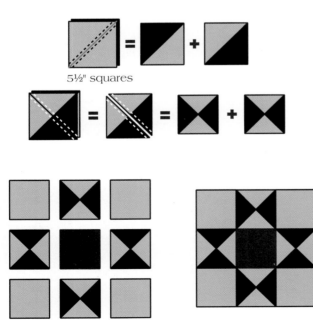

5½" squares

Fig. 3–5. Black/gold Variable Star

Sewing

The STARS, SPOOLS AND CHECKS wallhanging contains the Variable Star on point within the design. The quilt is assembled in three sections, a center diagonal row to which two triangular sections are added.

SPOOL BLOCKS

★ To make a template for the borders that surround the center square of the Spool block, trace the full-size template on page 55 or draw a 3½" x 10¼" rectangle on tracing paper. Cut out the rectangle. Fold the two top corners down to meet the lower edge to create 45° angles at each end of the rectangle. Cut away the triangles at the folds. Paste the wedge to template plastic and cut out the template shape.

★ Use the wedge-shape border template to cut 12 wedges from the 3½" gold strips and 12 from the 3½" green strips. Alternate placing the template on one edge and then the other along the strip for the most efficient use of fabric (Fig. 3–4a).

★ Border each of the 3½" black print squares with two green and two gold wedges, sewn opposite each other (b).

★ For the seams between the wedges and the squares, press allowances toward the outer edges. Press all the seam allowances between wedges in the same direction, either right or left (c).

BLACK/GOLD VARIABLE STAR

★ Use two 5½" black print squares and two 5½" gold squares to make four black/gold quarter-squares that measure 4¾" with seam allowances when completed.

★ Sew the black/gold quarter-squares with four 4¾" gold squares and one 4¾" black-print print center square to complete the star block (Fig. 3–5, page 48).

BLACK/GOLD/RED VARIABLE STAR

Half-squares

★ Make two half-squares from one 5⅛" red square and one 5⅛" gold square for two of the corners (Fig. 3–6).

Quarter-squares

★ Make two black-print/red star-point units from one 5½" black print square and one 5½" red square. The quarter-squares should measure 4¾" with seam allowances (Fig. 3–7).

Tri-color quarter-squares

★ Make the black-print/gold/red star-point units as follows:

★ Sew the 3" x 5½" red rectangles to the same-size gold rectangles to make two red/gold squares (5½"). Cut squares in quarters diagonally.

★ Cut one 5½" black-print square in quarters diagonally. Sew the red/gold quarters to the black print quarters to make two quarter-squares that measure 4¾" (Fig. 3–8).

★ Sew the star points, half-squares, and two 4¾" red squares together to complete the Variable Star block (Fig. 3–9).

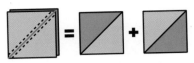

Fig. 3–6. Half-squares

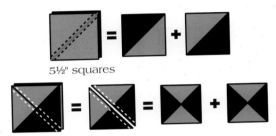

Fig. 3–7. Quarter-squares

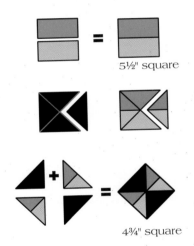

Fig. 3–8. Tri-color quarter-squares

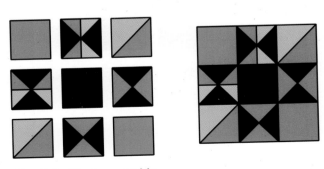

Fig. 3–9. Block assembly

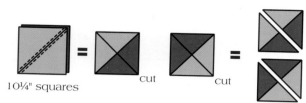

10¼" squares

Fig. 3–10. Two-color triangle

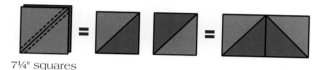

7¼" squares

Fig. 3–11. Half-squares

Two-color triangles

★ To make the green/gold triangles that frame the black/gold/red star, place a 10¼" gold square on a 10¼" green square, right sides together.

★ Draw a diagonal line on the wrong side of the top square. Stitch ¼" on both sides of the drawn line, then cut on the drawn line. Press the half-squares open.

★ Cut the half-squares from corner to corner, opposite the diagonal seam, to make four two-color triangles. Three of these units will be sewn to the black/gold/red star during quilt assembly. There will be one extra unit (Fig. 3–10).

★ For the fourth side of the star, make two half-squares from one 7¼" red square and one 7¼" green square.

★ Sew the two half-squares, with the green sides together (Fig. 3–11).

CHECKERBOARD BORDERS

Border strips

★ Sew a 3½" black strip to each of the red/red-print/gold 3½" strips to make five sets of strips.

★ From the black/gold strips, cut 24 3½" slices. Sew the slices together to make two borders containing 12 slices each, reversing every other slice, for the left side and top of the quilt (Fig. 3–12).

★ From the black and red sewn strips, cut 7 3½" slices. From the black and red print strips, cut 17 3½" slices.

★ Sew the remaining two borders from these slices, as shown in the Quilt Assembly diagram (Fig. 3–14).

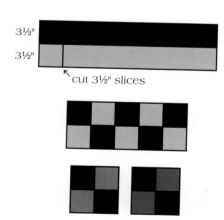

3½"

3½"

cut 3½" slices

Fig. 3–12. Making checkerboard borders

Checkerboard corners

★ Sew two black strips (2") alternating with two gold strips (2") (Fig 3–13). Cut the sewn strip into eight 2" slices. Sew the slices together, reversing every other slice, to make two of the corner blocks.

★ From the remaining 2" strips, cut 16 2" black squares, 10 2" red print squares, and six 2" red squares. Use these squares to make the other two checkerboard corners.

★ Sew the borders and checkerboard corners to the quilt.

Quilt assembly

★ Cut two 10¼" red squares and one 10¼" green square in quarters diagonally.

★ Following the Quilt assembly diagram (Fig. 3–14), lay out all the spool blocks, star blocks, two-color triangles, and quarter triangles, in order, on a flat surface. Sew the center diagonal row first.

★ Sew four red and four green quarter triangles together in pairs, two with the red triangle on the left and two with it on the right.

★ Sew quarter-square triangles together to make one green/gold quarter-square block.

★ Use the two-color triangles and the blocks to make the two corner sections of the quilt. Sew the corner sections and the center diagonal row together to complete the body of the quilt.

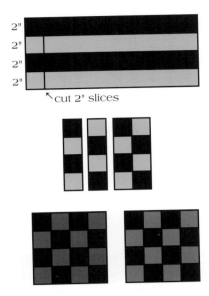

Fig. 3–13. Making checkerboard corners

Fig. 3–14. Quilt assembly

FINISHING

Layer the quilt with batting and backing. The quilt in the photo on page 46 has been machine quilted in a meandering pattern with black, red, and gold variegated thread. Bind the raw edges of the quilt with 2" continuous, double-fold bias binding.

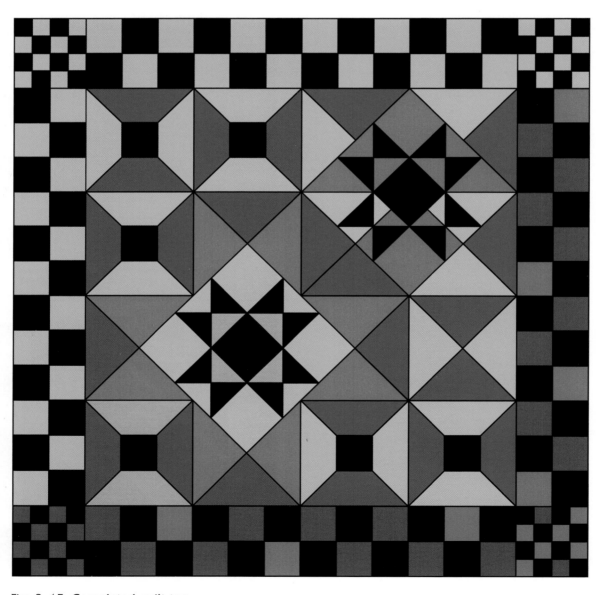

Fig. 3–15. Completed quilt top

Spool Block

Use this wedge-shaped template to cut borders for the squares to make Spool blocks. Instructions are on page 48.

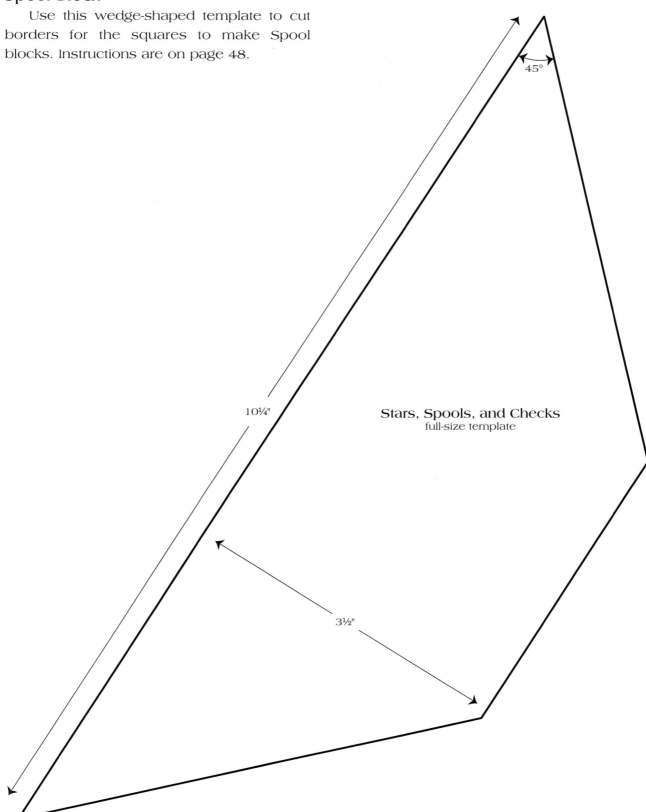

45°

10¼"

Stars, Spools, and Checks
full-size template

3½"

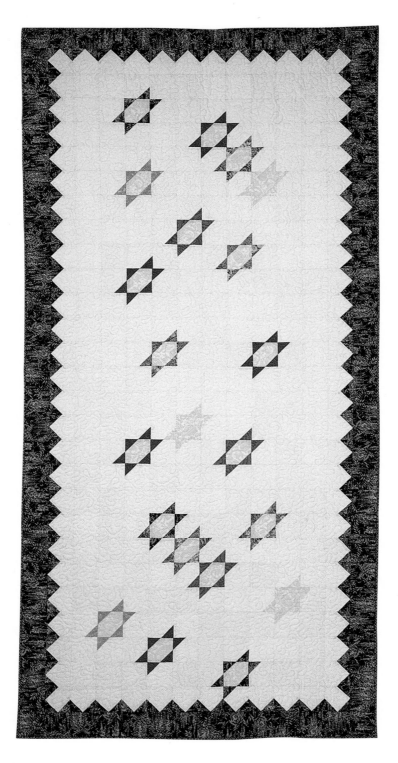

XQUISITE, 41½" x 92½", stairwell hanging made by Susan Denniston
and quilted by Vi Russell. This design can be used in quilts in many
sizes. Try changing color values for a fun color challenge.

SEW MANY STARS - *Gail Searl*

Chapter 4

Corner-Squares

The corner-square technique provides useful blocks for quilts. The large unpieced areas of the nine-patch Snowball, the Octagon, and the Square-Within-a-Square provide ample room for quilting designs. The three geometric shapes provide linkage between patterned blocks and promote the diagonal movement of the block patterns. Additionally, the Square-Within-a-Square can be used as a speed technique to produce pre-sewn units for other designs.

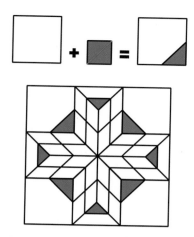

Fig. 4–1. One corner, Blazing Star block

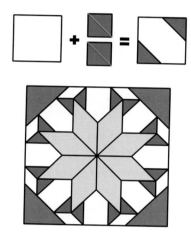

Fig. 4–2. Two corners, Gold Fish block

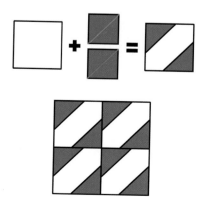

Fig. 4–3. Two corners, Indian Hatchet block

One corner: There are block patterns that utilize the corner-square technique to replace only one corner of a square within the block design, such as the squares that form the background of the Blazing Star pattern (Fig.4–1).

Two corners: A block design that replaces two corners of individual squares "on point" can be found in the Gold Fish block (Fig.4–2).

A one-patch design that replaces two corners is the Indian Hatchet (Fig.4–3).

Four corners: The most common use of the corner-square technique is when all four corners of the square are "rounded." Three block designs, the nine-patch Snowball, Octagon, and Square-Within-a-Square, may use the same technique. The difference among the three block patterns is the degree to which the corners of the square are "rounded," i.e., replaced, which depends on the size of the corner triangles (Fig.4–4).

Corner-square technique

The "rounding" of the corners of the square is common in designs. An easy way to make the triangles at the corners follows:

★ Place a small square face down in the corner of a larger square. Lightly draw a diagonal line, from corner to corner, on the back of the small square.

★ Sew one needle-width away, toward the corner, from the diagonal line.

★ Leaving a ¼" seam allowance, cut away the extra fabric at the corner (Fig.4–5).

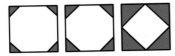

Fig. 4–4. Snowball, Octagon, Square-Within-a-Square

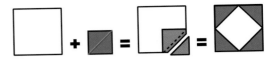

Fig. 4–5. Corner-square

Economical corner triangles

☆ ☆ ☆

For a more economical way to sew a corner triangle, use a template as a guide for positioning a half-square triangle in the corner instead of a square.

★ Start with a square cut from template plastic that is ⅛" larger than the short side of the finished corner triangle. Draw lines corner to corner on both diagonals in the square. Cut the square in half on one of the diagonals. Use one of the halves as your placement guide.

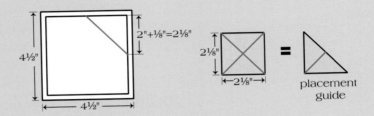

★ Cut a fabric square ⅞" larger than the short side of the finished corner triangle. On the wrong side of the fabric, draw both diagonals as you did for the template. Cut the fabric square in half on one of the diagonals to make two corner triangles.

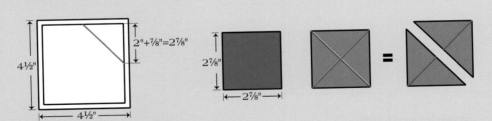

★ To use the guide, place it in the corner of a larger square. Then place the fabric triangle face down on the square, next to the guide, as shown below. Match the diagonal line on the fabric with line on the guide.

★ Sew the triangle to the square with a ¼" seam allowance. Cut off the extra fabric in the corner, leaving a ¼" seam allowance.

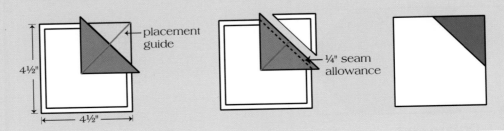

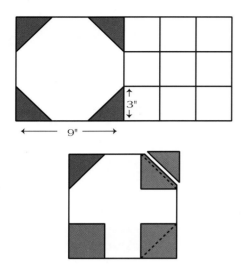

Fig. 4–6. Snowball block

DRAWING THE SNOWBALL BLOCK

The size of the corner triangles for a Snowball block are usually based on the grid of the neighboring block. *Example:* If the Snowball block alternates with a Nine Patch block that finishes 9", the short sides of the Snowball's corner triangles will be 3" (finished) to match the Nine Patch grid (Fig. 4–6).

★ To determine the size of the squares needed for the corner-square method, add ½" for seam allowances to the finished short side of the triangle. *Example:* For a 9" Snowball block with 3" corner triangles, the corner-square size would be 3½". (The Nine Patch and Snowball blocks measure 9½" before they are sewn together.)

DRAWING THE OCTAGON BLOCK

First, draw a square the size of the block needed (Fig. 4–7).

★ Draw an X from corner to corner inside the square. Measure the distance from one corner to the center of the X.

★ Set a compass to this measurement (or mark the distance on the edge of a sheet of paper). Place the point of the compass in each corner of the square and mark small arcs on each side of the square.

★ Connect the marks across each corner to complete the Octagon.

★ Measure the short side of the Octagon's corner triangles and add ½" for seam allowances to find the size of the square to use for the corner-square technique.

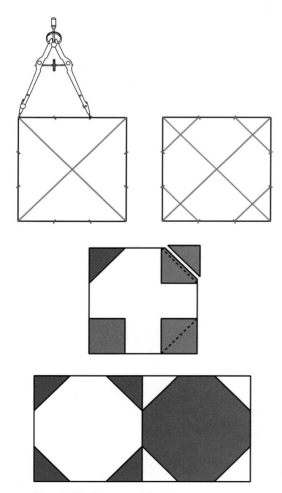

Fig. 4–7. Octagon block

Drawing the Square-Within-a-Square

You can determine the size of the corner-squares needed for the Square-Within-a-Square block just as you did for the Snowball and Octagon blocks. Another way to arrive at this measurement is to divide the size of the Square-Within-a-Square by 2 and add ½" for seam allowances. *Example:* A block that finishes 4" will need corner-squares that measure 2½" (4" divided by 2 equals 2", plus ½" equal 2½").

The versatile Square-Within-a-Square

The Square-Within-a-Square (Fig. 4–8) can be cut into units for making Sawtooth Stars, border designs, sashing strips, Flying Geese, and the three-piece Bonus Triangle.

Sawtooth Star

The Sawtooth Star is a four-patch design that assumes many disguises: The Sawtooth Star with a four-patch center is called "Indian Star." When the Sawtooth is grouped two across and two down, the design is known as "Devil Claws." (Notice that a grouping of four stars creates a fifth star in the center.)

The "Ribbon Star" is a fool-the-eye, positive-negative variation of the Sawtooth Star, which depends on dark star-points alternating with light star points. The Ribbon Star can be used as a horizontal and vertical lattice.

A two-color Sawtooth Star set on point creates a double lattice across the face of a quilt. When reduced in size, a nine-patch of Sawtooth Stars set on point will make a horizontal and vertical grid of stars.

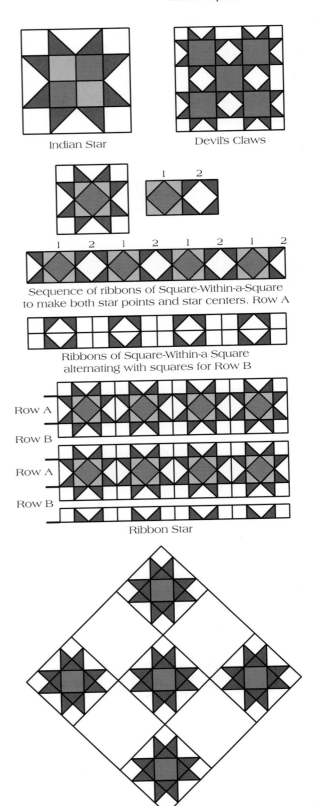

Indian Star

Devil's Claws

Sequence of ribbons of Square-Within-a-Square to make both star points and star centers. Row A

Ribbons of Square-Within-a-Square alternating with squares for Row B

Row A
Row B
Row A
Row B

Ribbon Star

Sawtooth Stars on point make a horizontal and vertical grid of stars on the face of the quilt

Fig. 4–9. Sawtooth Star variations

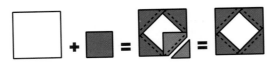

Fig. 4–8. Square-Within-a-Square

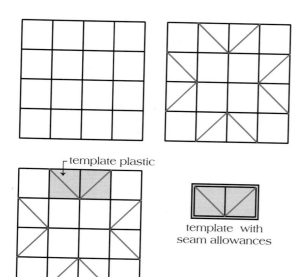

template plastic

template with
seam allowances

Fig. 4–10. Sawtooth Star grid

Drawing a Sawtooth Star: The Sawtooth Star is based on a 4 x 4 grid.

★ First draw a square the size of the block you need, minus seam allowances. Divide each side of the square into four divisions and connect the lines across the block to mark the grid .

★ Draw the center square by enclosing the four center grid squares and add the star-points as shown (Fig. 4–10).

★ Draw the star-points by creating right-side-up "V's" between the first and third division lines on each side of the square.

Turn-About Sawtooth Star: With this technique, you can make the star-points and the center square for a Sawtooth Star block from a Square-Within-a-Square (Fig.4–11).

★ Start by making a Square-Within-a-Square (Fig.4–12a). The first set of cuts are measured from the midline (b and c). The second set are measured from the edges of the block (d), or for greater accuracy, place template plastic over the drafted star. Trace around the three-piece star-point unit. Add ¼" seam allowances to the template.

★ Reverse each Flying-Geese unit, as shown in 4–12e, to make the star-points, which will be sewn to the center square cut from the Square-Within-a-Square.

★ From another fabric, cut four new squares for the corners of the Sawtooth Star block (f).

★ Sew the center square, squares, and star-points together to complete the block.

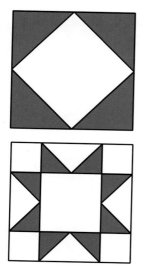

Fig. 4–11. Turn-About Sawtooth Star

Measuring the
Turn-About Sawtooth Star

⭐ ⭐ ⭐

You can make a Turn-About Sawtooth Star any size by using the following formulas to make the Square-Within-a-Square:

★ The Square-Within-a-Square equals the finished size of the Sawtooth Star block plus 2½". For example: to make an 8" Sawtooth Star, start with a 10½" square.

★ The applied corner squares equal half the Square-Within-a-Square plus ¼". For example: if the Square-Within-a-Square is 10½", the corner square is 10½ divided by 2, which equals 5¼", plus ¼" equals 5½".

★ The first cut, to the right and left of center, is half the corner square minus ½". For example: half of 5½" equals 2¾", minus ½" equals 2¼".

★ The second cut, measured from the outside edges, is half the corner square minus ¼". For example: half of 5½" equals 2¾", minus ¼" equals 2½".

★ The new corner-squares are equal to the short side of the Flying Geese unit. For example: the Flying Geese unit for the 8" Sawtooth Star is 2½" x 4½", so the new corner-squares are 2½" x 2½" (includes seam allowances).

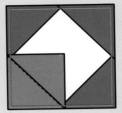

a. 10½" Square-Within-a-Square with 5½" corner-squares

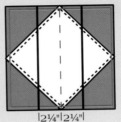

b. first cuts, measured from center

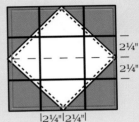

c. first cuts, opposite direction

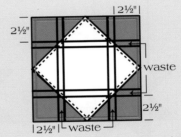

d. second cuts, measured from outside edge

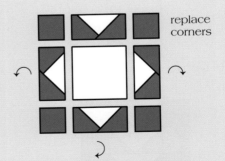

replace corners

e. turn-about the Flying Geese units

f. 2½" new corner-squares

Fig. 4–12. Turn-About Sawtooth Star

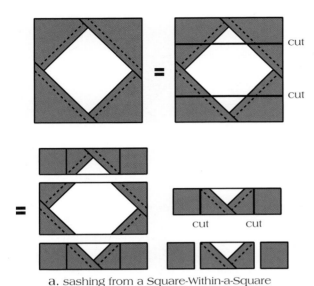

a. sashing from a Square-Within-a-Square

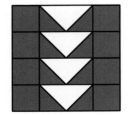

b. sashing forms a Sawtooth Star

c. use leftovers in other projects

Fig. 4–13. Sawtooth sashing

Sawtooth sashing. Sawtooth sashing can be made by applying the corner-square method to a rectangle, but it can also be made from the Square-Within-a-Square, as follows (Fig.4–13):

★ Make all the Square-Within-a-Square blocks the same size as the blocks to be sashed, including seam allowances.

★ Cut a strip the width of the sashing needed, with seam allowances, through the center of each square-within-a-square block (a).

★ When a setting square is added at the junction of four sashing strips made with the corner-square technique, the Sawtooth Star appears (b).

★ From the leftover pieces, you can cut four squares and two Flying-Geese units to use in other projects (c).

Three-piece bonus triangle. This triangle contains a square on point with a triangle sewn to two sides of the square.

The Square-Within-a-Square needs to be 1¼" larger than the long side of the finished Bonus Triangle.

A Square-Within-a-Square cut diagonally twice yields four Bonus Triangles (Fig. 4–14).

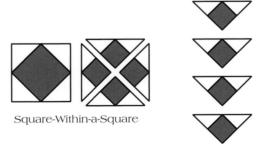

Square-Within-a-Square

Fig. 4–14. Bonus triangles

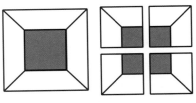

bordered square

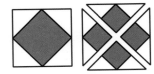

Square-Within-a-Square

Fig. 4–15. Make other blocks using bordered squares
and bonus triangles

More uses for the
Square-Within-a-Square

☆ ☆ ☆

When cut in four pieces, the Square-Within-a-Square can produce a wedge shape for borders (a).

The Square-Within-a-Square can also be used to make successive columns of Church Window blocks (b).

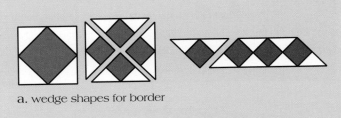

a. wedge shapes for border

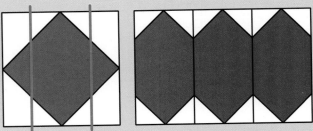

b. Church Windows using center of Square-Within-a-Square

XQ<small>UISITE</small> Wallhanging, 51" x 51", pieced by Laura Landstad and quilted by Vi Russell. For another version of XQuisite, see the XQuisite stairwell hanging on page 54.

XQUISITE
51" x 51"

XQuisite star block

★ ★ ★
corner-squares
p. 66

Materials	Yds.	First cut		Second cut	
		Cut strips selvage to selvage. Be sure to label all your pieces with their cut sizes.			
Lt. brown	1¾	15 strips	3½"	169 squares	3½"
Med. brown BORDER	1¼	10 strips	3½"	120 squares	3½"
STAR-POINTS fat quarter each					
Dk. brown		2 strips	2"	36 squares	2"
Rust/brown print		3 strips	2"	54 squares	2"
Rust		2 strips	2"	24 squares	2"
Med. orange print		2 strips	2"	24 squares	2"
Lt. orange print		2 strips	2"	30 squares	2"
Backing	3¼	2 panels	28" x 55"		
Binding	½				
Batting		55" x 55"			

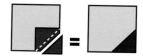

Fig. 4–16. star-points

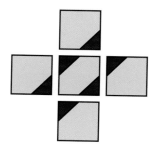

Fig. 4–17. Lay out the star

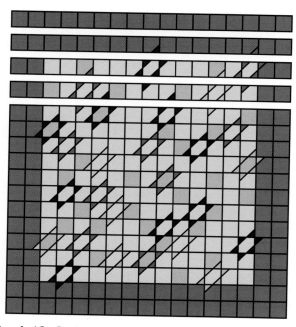

Fig. 4–18. Quilt assembly

Sewing

The Xquisite star can have many variations. Traditionally, the star pattern is an all-over design that utilizes scraps. Interesting variations can be found by varying the values of the background and the star-points to make the easy design into a challenging color exercise.

XQUISITE STARS

On an eye-level flannel board, place the 3½" background squares in 13 rows across and 13 down. Place two rows of medium brown "border" squares around the background squares.

★ Determine the position of the stars by randomly placing 28 of the 2" squares (star-points) on the background squares. Rearrange the star point squares until satisfied. Add a second star-point square to the background squares.

★ Place the star-point squares face down on diagonally opposite corners of the background fabric squares. Sew diagonally across the 2" squares. Allow a ¼" seam allowance and cut away the waste triangles to complete the star centers (Fig. 4–16).

★ Place four 2" squares face down on the four background squares adjacent to each of the star centers. Sew a diagonal seam across the 2" squares and cut off the waste triangles to create the four remaining star-points (Fig. 4–17).

★ Sew the squares together from left to right to make 17 rows. Press the seam allowances, alternating directions in each row to make it easier to match seams when joining the rows.

★ Sew the rows together from the top to the bottom (Fig. 4–18).

FINISHING

Layer the quilt with batting and backing, then quilt the layers. Bind the raw edges of the quilt with 2" continuous, double-fold bias binding.

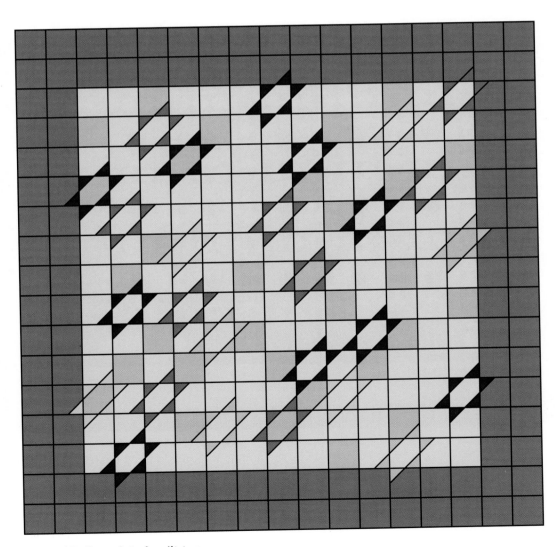

Fig. 4–19. Completed quilt top

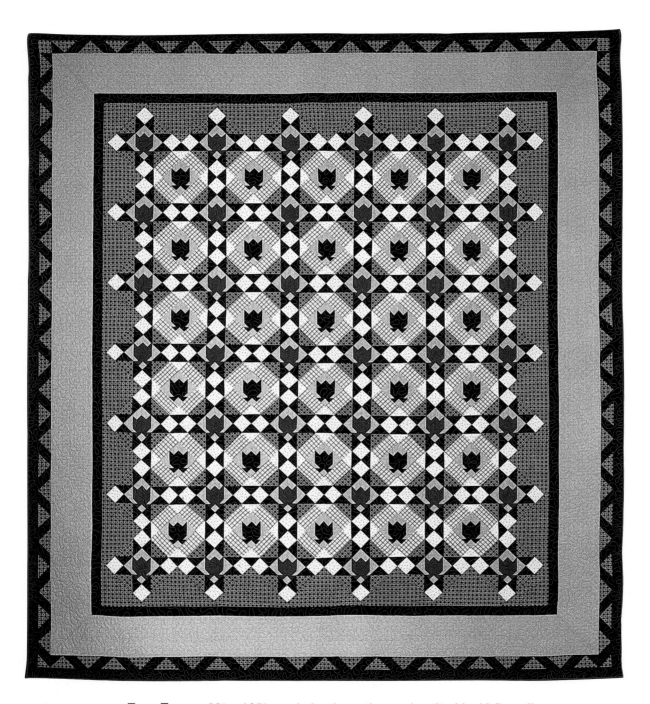

TULIP TRELLIS, 92" x 105", made by the author and quilted by Vi Russell.

TULIP TRELLIS
92" x 105"

30 Churn Dash Blocks, 8"

42 Sawtooth Stars, 8"

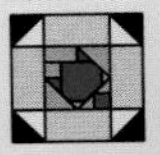

★ ★ ★

corner-squares
p. 70

Cut strips selvage to selvage. Be sure to label all your pieces with their cut sizes.

Materials	Yds.	First cut		Second cut	
Black	4¾				
TULIPS					
centers		3 strips	3"	30 squares	3"
logs 3 & 4		4 strips	2½"	strip piecing	
leaves		3 strips	1½"		
SAWTOOTH STAR		21 strips	2½"	336 squares	2½"
CHURN DASH		5 strips	2⅞"	60 squares	2⅞"
BORDER 1		8 strips	2"		
BORDER 3		12 strips	2½"	180 squares	2½"
BORDER 4		10 strips	2"		
		leftovers		1 square	2½"
Black Plaid	3¼				
SAWTOOTH STAR		19 strips	2½"	168 rectangles	2½" x 4½"
SIDE TRIANGLES		2 strips	14"	6 squares	14"
CORNER TRIANGLES		1 strip	7⅞"	2 squares	7⅞"
BORDER 3		10 strips	2½"	90 rectangles	2½" x 4½"
		leftovers		2 squares	2½"
		leftovers		1 square	2⅞"
White	1⅜				
SAWTOOTH STAR		11 strips	2½"	168 squares	2½"
CHURN DASH		5 strips	2⅞"	60 squares	2⅞"
Tan Plaid	1¼				
CHURN DASH		14 strips	2½"	120 rectangles	2½" x 4½"
Taupe	3⅝				
TULIPS					
log 1		6 strips	1"	72 rectangles	1" x 3"
log 2		6 strips	1"	72 rectangles	1" x 3½"
log 3		4 strips	1½"	strip piecing	
log 4		4 strips	2½"	strip piecing	
leaves		6 strips	1½"		
corner-squares		9 strips	2½"	144 squares	2½"
BORDER 2		9 strips	6¾"		
Blue	1⅝	3 strips	3"	42 squares	3"
Tulips					
logs 3 & 4		4 strips	2½"	strip piecing	
leaves		3 strips	1½"		
Binding		1 square	29"		
Backing	8⅜	3 panels	36" x 95"		
Batting		96" x 109"			

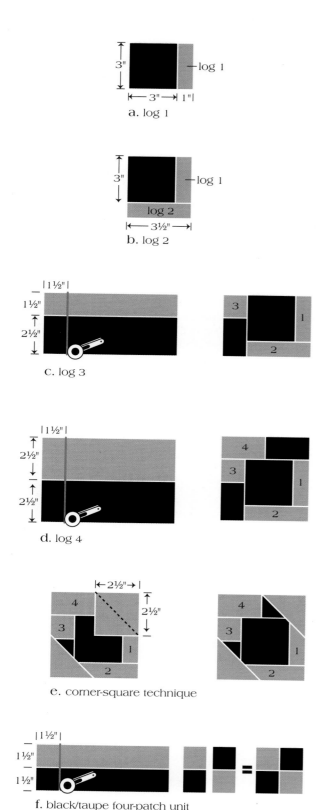

a. log 1

b. log 2

c. log 3

d. log 4

e. corner-square technique

f. black/taupe four-patch unit

Fig. 4–20a–f. Tulips, block assembly

Sewing

TULIP TRELLIS is designed with three blocks, the Sawtooth Star, Churn Dash variation, and Log Cabin Tulip. The lattice that frames the Churn Dash variation is created by placing the Sawtooth Star blocks on point.

BLOCK ASSEMBLY

Tulips: Part of the tulip block can be made by using the following Log Cabin technique (Fig. 4–20): (Use paper piecing for accuracy. See pattern on page 71.)

★ Log 1 (1" x 3" taupe) – Sew a log 1 to one side of each of the 30 3" black squares (a).

★ Log 2 (1" x 3½" taupe) – Add log 2 to each unit, overlapping log 1 (b).

★ Log 3 (1½" x 3½" black/taupe) – Make the Log 3 pieces by sewing a 2½" black strip to a 1½" taupe strip lengthwise. Make two black/taupe strips. Slice the strips into 1½" logs. Sew a log to each tulip unit as shown in c.

★ Log 4 (1½" x 4½" black/taupe) – Make two sets of sewn strips from the 2½" black strips and the 2½" taupe strips. Slice the sewn strips into 1½" logs. Sew a log to each tulip (d).

★ Use the corner-square technique (2½" taupe squares) to replace two corners of the Log Cabin tulip block as shown in e.

★ The tulip leaves are made from a four-patch unit, as follows: Sew a 1½" black strip to a 1½" taupe strip. Make a total of three black/taupe strips. Cut the strips into 1½" slices and sew pairs of slices together to make 30 black/taupe four-patch units (f).

★ Use the corner-square technique to sew a four-patch unit to each tulip (g).

★ Use the same techniques to make 42 blue/taupe tulips, substituting "blue" wherever the directions say "black."

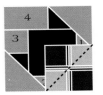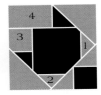

g. corner-square technique using four-patch unit

Fig. 4–20g. Tulips, block assembly

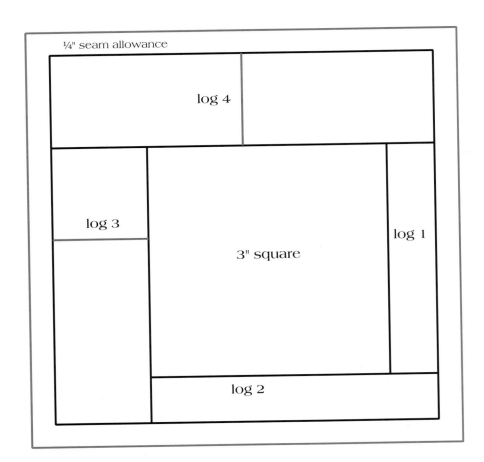

Fig. 4–21. Full-size pattern for paper piecing Tulip blocks.

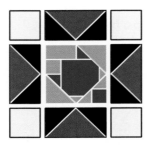

Flying Geese unit

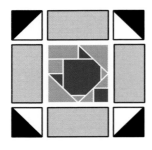

Fig. 4–22. Sawtooth Star assembly

2⅞" squares

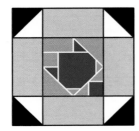

Fig. 4–23. Churn Dash variation assembly

Sawtooth Star

- ★ Using the corner-square technique, make 168 star-point (Flying Geese) units from the black plaid 2½" x 4½" rectangles and the 2½" black squares (Fig. 4–22).
- ★ Sew a star-point unit on two opposite sides of a blue tulip square.
- ★ Sew a 2½" white square to each end of two star-point units and sew the units to the tulip square to complete a Sawtooth Star block. Make 42 blocks.

Churn Dash variation

- ★ Use the 2⅞" white squares and 2⅞" black squares to make 120 black/white half-squares.
- ★ Sew a 2½" x 4½" tan-plaid rectangle to two opposite sides of the 42 black tulip squares.
- ★ Sew a black and white half-square to each side of 60 tan-plaid 2½" x 4½" rectangles. Sew these units to the tulip squares to complete the Churn Dash blocks (Fig. 4–23).

Setting triangles

- ★ Cut the 14½" black-plaid squares into quarters diagonally to make

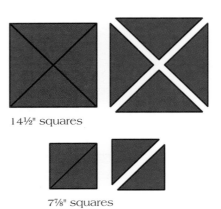

14½" squares

7⅞" squares

Fig. 4–24. Setting triangles

22 side triangles. There will be two extra triangles (Fig. 4-24).

★ Cut the 7⅞" black-plaid squares in half diagonally to make four corner triangles (Fig. 4–24).

QUILT ASSEMBLY

★ Arrange the Sawtooth Star blocks, Churn Dash blocks, and setting triangles on a flat surface in diagonal rows as shown in the quilt assembly diagram (Fig. 4–25).

★ Sew each diagonal row, then sew the rows together.

ADDING BORDERS

Border 1

★ Sew the 2" black strips, end to end with bias seams, to make the lengths needed for the border strips.

Border 2

★ Sew the 6¾" taupe border strips, end to end, with bias seams.

★ Sew the black Border 1 strips to the taupe Border 2 strips lengthwise. Cut the lengths needed for the borders and sew them to the quilt with mitered corners.

Border 3

★ Sew the remaining star-points, end to end, alternating them as shown in Fig. 4–26, to make the four border strips. You will need 21 starpoints for the top and bottom border strips and 24 star-points for the side border strips.

★ Cut two 2½" black plaid squares for the ends of the top border strip. Sew the squares in place (Fig. 4–26).

Fig. 4–25. Quilt assembly

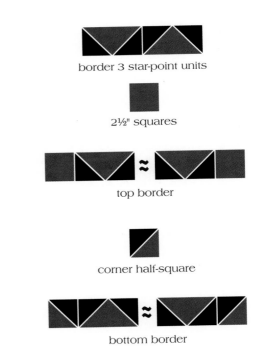

border 3 star-point units

2½" squares

top border

corner half-square

bottom border

Fig. 4–26. Border 3

★ Cut one 2⅞" black plaid square and one 2⅞" black square. Use these squares to make two half-squares. Sew the half-squares to the ends of the bottom border.

Note: It is not mathematically possible for the four corners to match.

★ Ease, pin, then sew the side border strips to the quilt first. Then add the top and bottom borders.

Border 4: Sew the black 2" strips together, end to end, with bias seams. Sew the borders to the quilt and miter the corners.

Finishing

Layer the quilt with batting and a backing, then quilt the layers. Bind the raw edges of the quilt with 2" continuous, double-fold bias binding.

Fig. 4–27. Completed quilt top

Fig. 4–28. Detail of borders, TULIP TRELLIS

PINK PEONY, 57½" x 74½", made by Sharon Goodrich.

PINK PEONY

57½" x 74½"

Jackson Star, 12" (medallion center)

Eight-Pointed Stars, 8½" (4 whole and 24 half stars)

★ ★ ★
bordered squares
p. 80

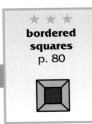

★ ★ ★
bonus triangles
p. 80

Cut strips selvage to selvage. Be sure to label all your pieces with their cut sizes.

Materials	Yds.	First cut		Second cut	
Dk. green	1				
Jackson Star		1 strip	1¾"	8 bias cuts	1¾" (45° diamonds)
Eight-Ptd. Stars		3 strips	4⅞"	17 squares	4⅞"
		2 strips	4"	11 squares	4"
		4 strips	2⅛"		
Lt. green	1				
Eight-Ptd. Stars		5 strips	2¹¹⁄₁₆"*	68 squares	2¹¹⁄₁₆"*
		10 strips	1¾"	40 rectangles	1¾" x 7¼"
Pink	⅛				
Eight-Ptd. Stars		2 strips	1¾"	8 pairs	1¾" (45° diamonds)
Red	2				
Jackson Star		1 strip	1¾"	8 pairs	1¾" (45° diamonds)
Eight-Ptd. Stars		12 strips	2¼"		
Medallion border		4 strips	3½" x 24¼"		
Binding		1 square	25"		
White	3½				
Border		7 strips	3½"		
Jackson Star		1 square	4"		
		8 squares	2¼"		
		4 rectangles	2¼" x 4"		
		2 squares	3¾"		
Background		1 rectangle	34½" x 51½"		
		3 squares	18¼"		
Backing	4⅜	2 panels	42" x 74"		
Binding	½				
Batting		61" x 78"			

A ruler marked in sixteenths is recommended.

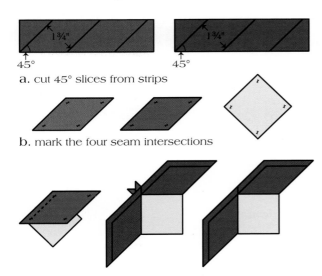

a. cut 45° slices from strips

b. mark the four seam intersections

c. sew from dot to dot, trim away the corners

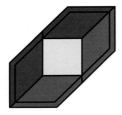

d. make the elongated hexagon

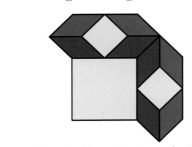

e. sew an elongated hexagon to each side

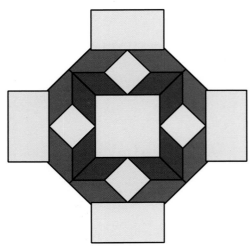

f. sew rectangles to the elongated hexagons

Fig. 4–29a–f. Jackson Star center

Sewing

Directions for the PINK PEONY include the bordered square and the bonus-triangle techniques. They are used for making the backgrounds of the red/green star blocks and "crowns" (half stars). The two techniques require accurate cutting and piecing to make this pattern fast and easy.

BLOCK ASSEMBLY

Jackson Star center

★ Use the cutting ruler's 45° angle to cut a beginning 45° angle on each of the 1¾" red strips and green strips.

★ Cut 1¾" 45° slices from the strips to make eight green diamonds and eight red diamonds (Fig. 4–29a).

★ Mark a dot (wrong side of fabric) at each of the four seam intersections on the 16 diamonds and on the corners of four of the 2¼" white on-point squares (b).

★ Sew two dark green diamonds to adjacent sides of each of the four squares. Sew two red diamonds to the opposite sides. Sew the red and the green diamonds to the squares from dot to dot. Do not sew into the seam allowances (c).

★ Fold square in half, edge to edge, to align the diamonds for mitering. Trim away the corners of the original square under diamonds.

★ Sew the red and green diamonds to each other, as if mitering, to make the elongated hexagons. Trim away the corners of the square below the diamonds (d).

★ Sew an elongated hexagon to each side of the 4" white center square, with the green diamonds touching the square. Miter the green diamonds at each corner (e).

★ Sew four 2¼" x 4" white rectangles to the elongated hexagons, which will stabilize the bias edges of the diamonds (f, page 78).

★ Press the green diamonds toward the center square. Press the red diamonds toward the rectangles. Set the center piece aside.

Pink crowns

★ Stitch two 1¾" pink strips together on one long side. Do not press the strips open.

★ Establish a beginning 45° angle for the sewn strips. Cut eight pairs of diamonds by making parallel 45° slices every 1¾" (Fig. 4–30a).

★ Cut two of the 3¾" white squares in an "X," from corner to corner, to make eight base triangles (b).

★ Use the following method to stitch two of the paired pink diamonds to each of the eight base triangles:

★ Align the 45° point of a pink diamond with the 45° angle of a base triangle. Sew from the tip of the diamond to the seam that joins the two diamonds. Stop. Pick out two stitches from the seam allowance so the second seam can be sewn.

★ Beginning at the diamond tip, sew the second diamond to the base triangle (c).

★ Stitch two diamond/base-triangle units to adjacent sides of each of the remaining 2¼" white squares. Miter the pink diamond units at the corner of the squares to create a four-diamond crown (d).

★ Sew the pink crowns to the red diamonds of the center piece and to the white rectangles to complete the Jackson Star block (e).

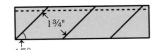

a. cut 45° slices from strips

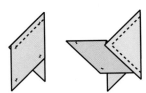

b. cut squares in an X to make base triangles

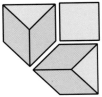
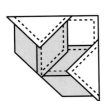

c. sew diamond to the base triangle

d. stitch diamond/base-triangle units to squares

e. sew the pink crown to the Jackson Star center

Fig. 4–30a–e. Jackson Star center with pink crowns

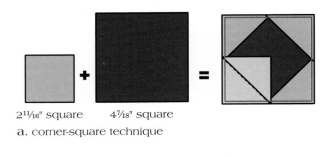

2¹¹⁄₁₆" square   4⅞" square

a. corner-square technique

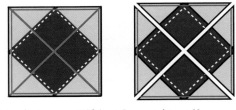

b. cut each Square-Within-a-Square in an X

Fig. 4–31. Bonus triangles

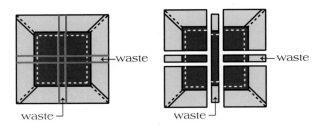

waste ←waste

waste—| waste—|

Fig. 4–32. Bordered-square units

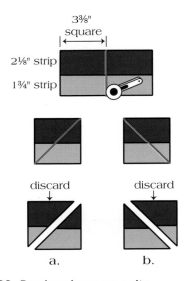

3⅜"
square
|←——→|

2⅛" strip

1¾" strip

discard   discard

a.   b.

Fig. 4–33. Bordered-square units

Green star and crown units

Bonus triangles

★ Use the corner-square technique to make 16 Square-Within-a-Square blocks from 16 4⅞" dark green squares and 64 2¹¹⁄₁₆" light green squares (Fig. 4–31a).

★ Cut each Square-Within-a-Square in an "X," from corner to corner. Set aside the 64 three-piece bonus triangles to use as base triangles in the stars and crowns (b).

Bordered-square units – Bordered-squares will be used to make the three-piece units at the center of each crown. Four of these units are also used in each star.

★ Use the 40 1¾" x 7½" light green rectangles to border the 4" dark green squares.

★ Turn a bordered square wrong side up. Place the 1½" line of the rotary ruler on the stitching line and cut across the square. Repeat on each side of the square to make four units. Discard the scraps. Make 40 of these units and set them aside (Fig. 4–32).

Strip-pieced units

★ Sew a light green 1¾" strip to a dark green 2⅛" strip lengthwise. Make four two-color strips (Fig. 4–33).

★ Cut 48 3⅜" squares from the strips. Place the squares with their light green edges on the bottom. Cut 24 of the squares in half diagonally from the lower left to the upper right. Discard upper-left triangles (a).

★ Cut the other 24 squares in half from the lower right to the upper left. Discard upper right triangles (b).

Red diamonds

★ Sew two red 2¼" strips along their length, with right sides facing, using a ¼" seam. Make a total of four pairs of strips. Do not press strips open.

★ Cut a 45° angle at the beginning of the strips. Cut 64 pairs of diamonds (2¼" wide) parallel to the 45° angle (Fig. 4–34).

Red/green stars and crowns

★ Sew a pair of red diamonds to each of the 64 three-piece base triangles (Fig. 4–35a).

★ Sew the diamond/base-triangle units together in pairs and add bordered-square and strip-pieced units to make 32 half stars (b).

★ Sew eight of the half stars together to make four whole Eight-Pointed Stars (c).

cut 45° diamonds from sewn strips

Fig. 4–34. Red diamonds

a. sew diamonds to bonus triangles

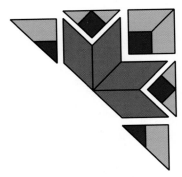

b. sew the units together to make half stars

c. sew four whole stars

Fig. 4–35. Red/green stars and crowns

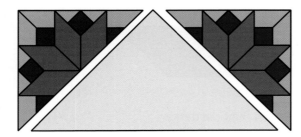

Fig. 4–36. Sew crown to short side of triangle

Fig. 4–37. Quilt assembly

QUILT-TOP ASSEMBLY

Sew the red/green crowns to each side of the Jackson Star.

★ Sew the 3½" red border strips to the Jackson Star medallion and miter the corners to complete the center design.

★ Fold the 34½" x 51½" white background fabric into fourths. Lightly press the folds to use as guides for positioning the center medallion.

★ Turn under the center medallion allowances and appliqué the center in place. (Optional: Cut away the background fabric beneath the medallion.)

BORDER ASSEMBLY

Cut the three 18¼" white background squares in quarters from corner to corner twice, like an X. Set aside two quarters to use in another project.

★ Sew a crown to the short sides of each triangle. Complete 10 rectangular units (Fig. 4–36).

★ Join three rectangles together for each side and sew these to the quilt top.

★ Sew two rectangles together, plus a whole corner star block at each end, for the top and for the bottom. Sew these borders to the quilt top.

★ Join the eight 3½" white border strips, end to end, as needed to make the borders. Sew the borders to the quilt top and miter the corners.

FINISHING

Layer the quilt with batting and a backing, then quilt the layers. Bind the raw edges of the quilt with 2" continuous, double-fold bias binding.

Fig. 4–38. Completed quilt top

Big Red, 76" x 92", made by the author and quilted by Vi Russell. The Sawtooth Star block (page 61) alternates with a Churn Dash block to make a diagonal grid on the quilt. Use the Corner-square and Half-square techniques to sew this scrap quilt.

SEW MANY STARS - *Gail Searl*

Chapter 5

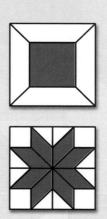

Perfectly Easy Miters

When mitered borders are cut prior to being sewn, the bias edges at the ends of the border strips can easily become distorted, making the borders difficult to sew. On the other hand, when border lengths are not cut to size, the finished square can be distorted in the attempt to find the miter line by folding one border length at a right angle against the other.

The perfect-miter technique solves the problem of uneven borders and provides the means to achieve a distortion-free mitered border. The method can be used for bordered squares as well as quilt tops.

2" + 4½" square + 2" = 8½"

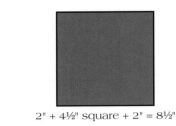

Fig. 5–1. Cut border 8½" for a 4½" square

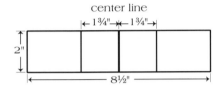

center line

|← 1¾"→|←1¾"→|

2"

8½"

Fig. 5–2. Mark miter placement

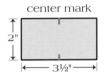

center mark

2"

|← 3½" →|

Fig. 5–3. Template is faster and more accurate

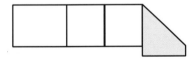

Fig. 5–4. Press diagonal creases to establish the miter line

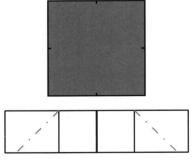

Fig. 5–5. Match center of the square and border strip

The perfect miter

The perfect-miter technique begins with a working border length, to provide ease for the "turn of the cloth" when mitering. The working border is trimmed after it is sewn. As an alternative method, you can pre-cut the miter to fit, as described on page 88.

★ The "working length" of a border is THE SIDE OF THE QUILT OR SQUARE (UNFINISHED), PLUS A WIDTH (UNFINISHED) OF THE CUT BORDER AT EACH END. *Example:* Cut a 2" (unfinished) border for a 4½" (unfinished) square, (2" + 4½" + 2" = 8½"). Be accurate. The miter seams depend on evenly cut borders.

★ Transfer the four working-length border strips to the ironing board. Mark the center of each strip within the seam allowance.

★ To find the miter placement, measure the side of the unfinished quilt or square. Subtract 1" from the measurement. Divide the result by 2. For the 4½" square, 4½" minus 1" = 3½" divided by 2 = 1¾". For the 4½" square, place a mark 1¾" to the right and 1¾" to the left of center. Draw a line across the width of the border strips at the marks (Fig. 5–2).

★ *Note:* When sewing several bordered squares, a template can be used to mark the center and the distances to the right and left of center. In the example, the template would be a rectangle 2" wide by 3½" in length with a mark at the center (Fig. 5–3).

★ Fold the upper-right and upper-left corners down at the drawn lines. The folds form flaps like "collie ears" (Fig. 5–4). Press. (The border ends will extend below the bottom edge of the strip.) Repeat the process for the remaining three border strips.

★ *Note:* By pressing the diagonal crease to establish the miter line, an allowance for the turn of the cloth at the seam has been made. Do not cut away the fabric that extends beyond the creased miter lines until the final pressing of the square.

★ Match the centers of the borders to the centers of the sides of the square. (Fig. 5–5).

★ Sew the border strip to the square, beginning one stitch in from the pressed miter line. Sew to within one stitch of the miter crease on the opposite side of the square (Fig. 5–6). Next, sew the border on the opposite side of the square, followed by the remaining two borders.

★ Fold the bordered square in half diagonally, right sides together. Open the flaps. Perfectly align the blunt ends of the strips and pin. Finger press all seam allowances toward the square.

★ Sew the miters in the crease, while keeping the blunt ends of the strips even (Fig. 5–7).

★ While the square is still folded diagonally, cut off the fabric that extends beyond the crease, leaving ¼" seam allowance (Fig. 5–8).

★ Press the mitered seams clockwise and the center square flat (Fig. 5–9).

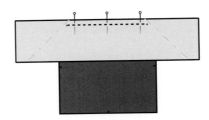

Fig. 5–6. Sew border strips to square

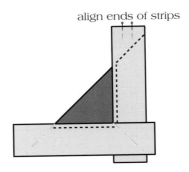

Fig. 5–7. Sew the miters in the crease

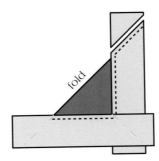

Fig. 5–8. Trim, leaving ¼" seam allowance

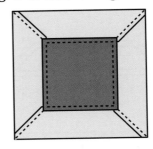

Fig. 5–9. Press mitered seams clockwise and center square flat

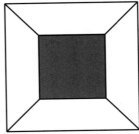

Fig. 5–10. Bordered square, with perfect miter

4" finished square

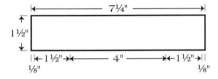

Fig. 5–11. Figure the length of the pre-cut mitered border

fold

template with seam allowance

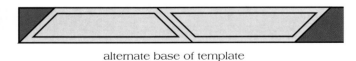
alternate base of template

Fig. 5–12. Make a template

The perfect pre-cut miter

The pre-cut mitered border is the most convenient border to use for patches or blocks. The seam allowances for the mitered corners are included in the pre-cut border.

★ The length of the pre-cut mitered border, unlike the working border, is the finished square plus the width of the unfinished border plus ⅛" at each end. *Example:* To border a 4" square (finished) with a 1½" border (unfinished), add 1½" (border width) at each end of the border to allow for the seam allowances at the mitered corners. Add ⅛" at each end to allow for the turn of the cloth. Thus, ⅛" + 1½" + 4" + 1½" + ⅛" = 7¼" (Fig. 5–11).

★ To make a template (Fig. 5–12) for the border in the example, fold the upper corners of a 1½" x 7¼" paper rectangle down to meet the base of the rectangle to create the 45° angle for mitering the borders. Cut off the triangles at each end. The template includes the seam allowances for mitering. Paste the paper pattern to template plastic and use the template to precut the borders. Sew the pre-cut borders and the miters with a ¼" seam allowance.

★ *Note:* You can stabilize the squares to be bordered with spray sizing. When cutting the borders, alternate the base of the template between the top and the bottom of the strip.

The easy-eight mitered star

The easy-eight is a four-patch, cut-easy-sew-easy star that is trouble free. It requires only the pre-cut-miter and the corner-square techniques for instant success.

★ To find the size of the square needed, determine the finished size of the block. Divide the finished size in half and add 1½" for seam allowances and cutting ease.

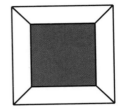

a. sew pre-cut borders to the square and miter corners

The easy-eight mitered star

☆ ☆ ☆

EXAMPLES

6" square

Finished size	Cut Square
6" divided by 2 = 3" + 1½" =	4½"

10" square

Finished size	Cut Square
10" divided by 2 = 5" + 1½" =	6½"

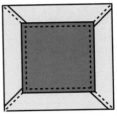

b. press frame seams clockwise and center square flat

★ Sew pre-cut borders to the square and miter the corners (Fig. 5–13a).

★ Turn the bordered square to the wrong side (b). Using the measurement for the inside cuts from the Easy-Eight Cutting Chart, place the ruler on a seam joining the border to the square. Align the ruler's horizontal lines with the seam lines of adjacent borders. Cut across the center of the square, dividing the square (c).

★ Repeat the measuring and cutting for the opposite side of the square. A scrap will remain in the center. Cut each piece again by aligning the ruler with the seams, as before. There will be scraps between these pieces also (d).

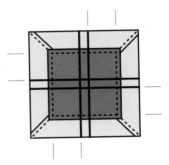

c. measure inside cuts from the seam line

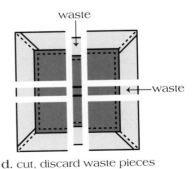

d. cut, discard waste pieces

Fig. 5–13a–d. Easy-eight Mitered Star

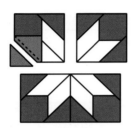

e. square cut from background fabric,
the same width as border

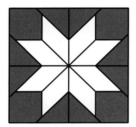

f. sew square on diagonals parallel
to the mitered seams

★ On one of the pieces, place a square of background fabric (cut the same size as the border width) (e).

★ Sew the background square to the piece with a diagonal seam, corner to corner. The diagonal seam across the square should be parallel to the mitered seams.

★ Cut off the waste triangles, leaving a ¼" seam allowance. Repeat for the other side of the piece (f).

★ Repeat for the other three quarters and press the units.

★ Turn the four units so the mitered corners will be in the center of the star block. Sew the block as a four patch, magically producing the easy eight-mitered star (g).

g. sew four quarters together

Fig. 5–13e–g. Easy-eight Mitered Star

Easy-Eight Cutting Chart

Finished Star Block	Working Square Cut Size (½ finished star + 1½")	Background Squares (¼ finished star + ½")	Pre-cut Border	Seamline Cuts* (¼ finished block + ¼")
6"	4½"	2"	2" x 8¼"	1¾"
8"	5½"	2½"	2½" x 10¼"	2¼"
10"	6½"	3"	3" x 12¼"	2¾"
12"	7½"	3½"	3½" x 14¼"	3¼"

* measure from border seams on the wrong side

AUNT ELIZA'S STAR, 46½" x 46½", made by Beaver Aspevig. This wallhanging uses Aunt Eliza's Stars and Wood Lily blocks. Techniques include strip-pieced diamonds, bordered-square star-points, and identical eighths.

FALLING STARS, 36" x 36", made by Pat Feeney and quilted by Pat Meldrum.

FALLING STARS
36" x 36"

Cube Lattice Blocks, 8"

★ ★ ★
**easy-eight
star points**
p. 94

Cut strips selvage to selvage. Be sure to label all your pieces with their cut sizes.

Materials	Yds.	First cut		Second cut	
Scraps		⅛ yd. each of 11 different fabrics for the star points and pieced border 1			
		leftovers		12 squares	3⅜"
				2 squares	1½"
Dk. Blue	2⅛	1 strip	7½"	2 rectangles	7½" x 15½"
		2 strips	5½"	11 squares	5½"
		1 strip	4½"	2 rectangles	4½" x 8½"
		leftovers		2 rectangles	4½" x 2½"
				2 squares	3⅜"
		6 strips	2½"	88 squares	2½"
Border 1		3 strips	1½"		
Border 2		4 strips	2½"		
Backing	1⅛	1 panel	40½" x 40½"		
Binding	½ (included in dark blue yardage)				
Batting		42" x 42"			

a. cut using 2½" x 10¼" template

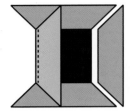

b. sew the borders to the square

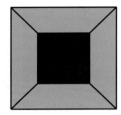

c. sew pre-cut borders to the
square and miter corners

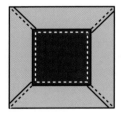

d. press seam allowances
clockwise

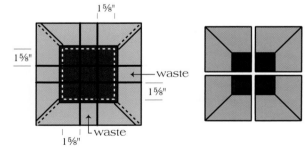

e. cut the bordered squares
into four star-point units

f. sew 2½" squares in opposite
corners parallel to seamline
to make star-points

Fig. 5–14a–f. Easy-eight star-points

Sewing

For the FALLING STARS wallhanging, use the easy-eight technique to make a four-patch star from a bordered square. The easy-eight technique provides rotary-cut, pre-pieced units instead of individual parallelograms for the star points, which makes the easy-eight a speed technique.

The Cube Lattice block, when pieced edge to edge, forms a repetitive star design. However, in FALLING STARS, whole and partial stars make the design.

The stars are made from ⅛ yard each of 11 different fabrics that range from green to gold to orange. The colors vary in hue and intensity.

TEMPLATE CONSTRUCTION

The borders for the 5½" dark blue squares can be pre-cut. Make a wedge-shaped template by drawing and cutting a 2½" x 10¼" paper rectangle. Cut 45° angles at each end. Paste the paper template to template plastic and cut out the template. Cut a 2½" strip from each star-point fabric and use the wedge template to cut four borders from each fabric (a). Alternate the base of the template from edge to edge along the strips.

EASY-EIGHT STAR-POINTS

★ Sew the pre-cut wedge borders to the 5½" dark blue squares. Sew opposite sides when applying the first two strips for an easy application (b).

★ Miter the corners (c). Trim the protruding tips from the mitered strips. Press the center square flat. Press the corner seam allowances clockwise (d).

★ Turn the bordered squares face down. Place the 2¼" line of the cutting ruler on the seam line that joins the border to the dark blue square. Slice across the bordered square.

★ Rotate bordered square to cut from each side. There will be some waste between the units. Cut all 11 bordered squares into accurate units (e).

★ Place two 2½" squares face down on each of the units. Sew the diagonals of the squares from the outside edge of the border to the inside edge of the applied squares (f).

★ Cut away the waste triangles. Fold back the applied squares to complete the star-points. (Two are extra.)

BORDERED RECTANGLES

A pieced border is sewn to the large 7½" x 15½" blue rectangles that appear at the lower left half and at the upper right half of the quilt.

★ Cut two 3⅜" dark blue squares and 14 3⅜" colored squares. Sew 16 half-squares. Arrange the half-squares into two horizontal rows of five half-squares ending with a blue/color half-square. Arrange the remaining half-squares into 2 vertical rows of 2 half-squares. Begin each vertical row with a blue/color half square. Sew the half-squares into 4 rows (Fig. 5–15).

★ Cut a 1½" strip along the middle (lengthwise) of the horizontal and vertical rows. Sew a 1½" dark blue strip to the blue end of the horizontal rows. Sew a 1½" dark blue strip to the blue end of the vertical rows and a 1½" colored square to the opposite end.

★ Complete by sewing the horizontal and the vertical strips to two adjacent sides of the 7½" x 15½" dark blue rectangles (Fig. 5–16).

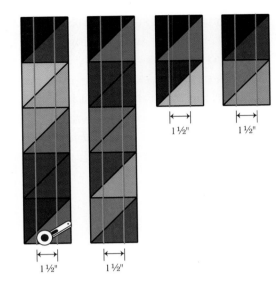

Fig. 5–15. Cut 1½" strip from the middle of each half-square strip

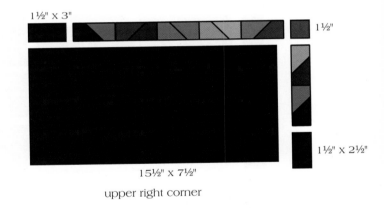

upper right corner

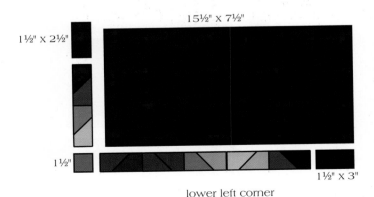

lower left corner

Fig. 5–16. Bordered rectangles upper right and lower left corners

QUILT ASSEMBLY

★ Arrange 21 star-point units for the left half of the wallhanging according to the quilt assembly diagram. Repeat the layout for the right half. Turn the right half upside down. (The left half of the wallhanging ends with the multicolored strip. The right half begins with the multi-colored strip.)

BORDER

Cut four 2½" x 37½" blue pre-cut borders. Center and sew the borders to the wallhanging. Sew the pre-cut mitered borders at each corner.

FINISHING

Layer the quilt with batting and a backing, quilt the layers together. Bind the raw edges of the quilt with 2" continuous, double-fold bias binding.

Fig. 5–17. Quilt assembly

Fig. 5–18. Completed quilt top

FALLING STARS, 68" x 86", made by Marjorie Chinadle and quilted by
Sandra McEwen. This twin-size quilt uses the Easy-Eight technique,
page 89 to make a four-patch star from a bordered-square.

Chapter 6

Eight-Pointed Stars

The 45° diamond used in sewing the Eight-Pointed Star has at least two sides that are cut on the bias as a result of the 45° angles. Joining eight diamonds with all the bias seams can become a problem. Other difficulties in sewing the star can be traced to inaccurate patterns or inaccurate measuring and cutting. The first step in successfully sewing the Eight-Pointed Star is to learn to draw one, which is really quite easy to do. You will be able to make these stars in any size.

a. 5" square

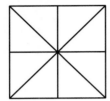

b. Draw an X in the square, draw horizontal and vertical lines

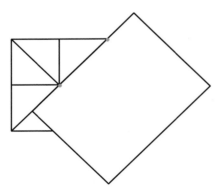

c. Mark dots at the corner and center on the edge of a piece of paper

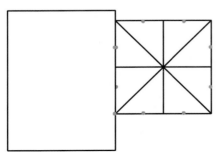

d. Place paper guide with one dot on the corner, mark the square where the other dot falls

e. Connect the dots to make an octagon

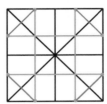

f. Connect the dots with two horizontal and two vertical lines

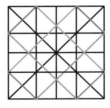

a = corner square
b = 1.414 x a for base triangle

g. Draw diagonal lines to complete the star

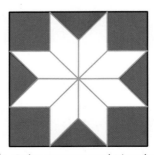

h. Color corners and triangles

Fig. 6–1. Drawing the Eight-Pointed Star

Drawing the Eight-Pointed Star

Draw a 5" octagon-shaped star.

★ Draw a 5" square (Fig. 6–1a). Draw an X from corner to corner. Draw the horizontal and vertical center lines to divide the square into eight sections (b).

★ Use a compass or the edge of a sheet of paper to make dots to mark the *distance from the center of the square to one of the corners* (c).

★ Use a compass or use the edge of a sheet of paper to mark the distance from the center fo the square to one of the corners.

★ With each corner of the square as a fulcrum, mark this *center-to-corner distance* on each side of the square (d). Begin at the upper-left corner and work clockwise. Then reverse directions, moving around the square in a counter-clockwise direction. When finished, there will be two dots on each side of the square near the corners.

★ Connect the dots across the corners to make an octagon (e).

★ Connect the dots across the square with two vertical lines and two horizontal lines (f).

★ Draw two sets of diagonal lines to complete the star (g).

★ Color the small squares at each corner and the triangles at the midpoint of each side to outline the star (h).

SEWING EIGHT-POINTED STARS

To sew an Eight-Pointed Star with ease, first draw the star in the size you want, then find the measurements required. Three measurements are needed: (1) the size of the squares at the corners of the star block, (2) the width of the star points, and (3) the length of the base of the triangle separating the star points. Add seam allowances.

Note: Eight-Pointed Stars usually have measurements using sixteenths of an inch. A ruler with sixteenths is recommended.

NO-FAIL MACHINE PIECING

The no-fail technique for machine-piecing stars begins with presewn pairs of star points, which are used to form quarter units of the star. The star is then assembled as a four-patch. This technique avoids most of the problems encountered in sewing individual diamonds to make stars. As a bonus, the paired diamonds do not require pinning. The seam allowances at the center of the back of the star form a square, not a star.

Measuring and cutting

★ Measure the width of the diamond star point, as shown in Fig. 6–2a.

★ Cut two strips of fabric, selvage to

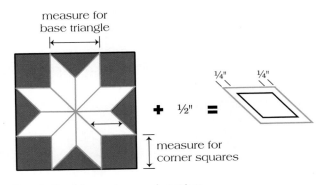

Fig. 6–2a. Measuring and cutting

b. sew strips together

width of star point plus ½" seam allowance

c. cut 45° slices from strip

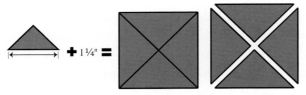

d. cut a square that is 1¼" larger than measurement

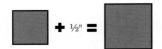

e. measure corner squares and add ½" for seam allowance

Fig. 6–2b–e. Measuring and cutting

pick out 3 stitches at V

a. press diamonds open

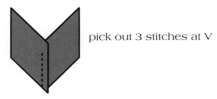

b. sew triangle into the "V" of the joined diamonds

c. press seams

Fig. 6–3a–d. Sew triangles to the star-points

selvage, the width of the star points plus ½" for seam allowances. Sew the two strips together, right sides facing, along one edge (b).

★ Lay the strips on a cutting mat with the seam on the upper edge. Align the 45° line of the ruler with the bottom edge of the strips and cut 45° slices the width of the cut strips with the rotary cutter. (c).

★ For the base triangles, measure the long side of a triangle in your drawing. Cut a square that is 1¼" larger than that measurement (d). Cut four base triangles by cutting the square diagonally twice like an X.

★ Measure the corner-squares in the drawing. Add ½" for seam allowances and cut four corner-squares (e).

Star-points and triangles

★ Pick out three stitches from the V of the paired diamonds (Fig. 6-3a).

★ Match the paired diamonds to the base triangles. The edges of the diamonds will exactly match the short sides of the base triangles (b).

★ There's no need to pin. Sew the edge of one diamond to the base triangle by sewing from the base to the top of the triangle, stopping ¼" from the edge (c). Align the second diamond with the base triangle and sew as before.

★ Press the seam allowances of the diamonds and the base triangles in one direction for all four diamond/base-triangle units (d). Use the tip of the iron only.

Attaching squares

★ Sew two diamond/base-triangle units to adjacent sides of a square as if mitering. Stitch to within ¼" from the corner.

★ The resulting unit looks like a four-pointed crown. Sew a second four-pointed crown in the same manner.

★ Sew both crowns to the two remaining squares. (Fig. 6–4).

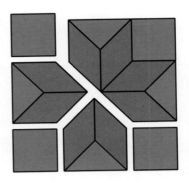

Fig. 6–4. Attach squares

Joining halves

★ Use a pin to match the centers of the halves. Remove the pin. Use five or six long stitches to stay-stitch the center seams (Fig. 6-5a). Verify a perfect match at the center.

★ Return to the regular stitch length and sew from one corner to the opposite corner (b).

★ Pick out two stitches from the seam allowances at the center. Press the seam allowances with the tip of the iron to form a square at the center of the star. The center will form a square, not a star, because the diamonds were joined as quarters instead of as individual diamonds, as is done in hand sewing (c).

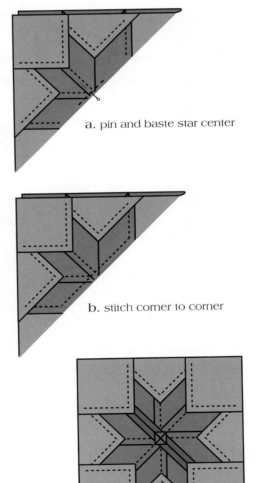

a. pin and baste star center

b. stitch corner to corner

c. seam allowances will form a square in the center

Fig. 6–5a–c. Join halves

CHRISTMAS WITH RIBBONS, 64" x 64", made by Pat Meldrum.

CHRISTMAS WITH RIBBONS
64" x 64"

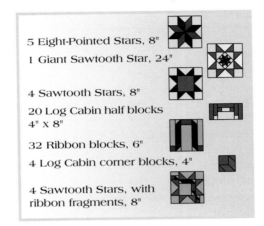

5 Eight-Pointed Stars, 8"

1 Giant Sawtooth Star, 24"

4 Sawtooth Stars, 8"

20 Log Cabin half blocks
4" x 8"

32 Ribbon blocks, 6"

4 Log Cabin corner blocks, 4"

4 Sawtooth Stars, with
ribbon fragments, 8"

★ ★ ★

**eight-pointed
stars**
p. 107

Cut strips selvage to selvage. Be sure to label all your pieces with their cut sizes.

Materials	Yds.	First cut		Second cut	
Lt. Gold	½				
GIANT SAWTOOTH STAR		2 strips	6½"	4 rectangles	6½" x 12½"
		leftovers		4 squares	6½"
Med. Gold	1¾				
EIGHT-POINTED STARS		2 strips	2⅞"	20 squares	2⅞"
		1 strip	4½"	5 squares	4½"
SAWTOOTH STARS		2 strips	2½"	16 rectangles	2½" x 4½"
		1 strip	2½"	16 squares	2½"
SETTING TRIANGLES		1 strip	7¼"	2 squares	7¼"
ACCENT BLOCKS		2 strips	8½"	8 squares	8½"
LOG CABIN BORDER		3 strips	2½"	20 rectangles	2½" x 4½"
		1 strip	2½"	strip piecing	
		2 strips	1½"	strip piecing	

CHART CONTINUES ON PAGE 106.

CHART CONTINUES FROM PAGE 105.

Cut strips selvage to selvage. Be sure to label all your pieces with their cut sizes.

Materials	Yds.	First cut		Second cut	
Dk. Gold	2				
RIBBON BORDER		5 strips	2½"	32 rectangles	2½" x 5½"
		5 strips	1½"	136 squares	1½"
		3 strips	5½"	strip piecing	
		1 strip	3½"	4 squares	3½"
		2 strips	2½"	16 rectangles	2½" x 4½"
		leftovers		6 squares	1⅞"
		leftovers		8 rectangles	1½" x 2½"
		leftovers		8 squares	2½"
		10 strips	1½"	spliced strips	
Red	½				
EIGHT-POINTED STARS		2 strips	2⅛"	strip piecing (diamonds)	
RIBBON BORDER		3 strips	1½"	36 rectangles	1½" x 2½"
		3 strips	1½"	strip piecing	
		leftovers		8 squares	1½"
Red Print	⅞				
EIGHT-POINTED STARS		2 strips	2⅛"	strip piecing (diamonds)	
SAWTOOTH STARS		2 strips	2½"	32 squares	2½"
RIBBON BORDER		11 strips	1½"	64 rectangles	1½" x 6½"
		leftovers		4 rectangles	1½" x 4½"
		leftovers		6 squares	1⅞"
Teal	½				
LOG CABIN CORNER		1 strip	2⅛"	strip piecing (star points)	
ACCENT BLOCKS		2 strips	6½"	8 squares	6½"
Teal Print	1⅜				
GIANT SAWTOOTH STAR		2 strips	6½"	8 squares	6½"
LOG CABIN BORDER		2 strips	1½"	strip piecing	
		7 strips	1½"	60 rectangles	1½" x 4½"
		2 strips	3½"	strip piecing	
LOG CABIN CORNERS		leftovers		4 squares	2⅞"
		leftovers		4 squares	2⅛"
RIBBON BORDER		2 strips	2½"	32 squares	2½"
SAWTOOTH STARS		leftovers		4 squares	4½"
Backing	4	2 panels	34½" x 68"		
Binding	½				
Batting		68" x 68"			

Sewing

The CHRISTMAS WITH RIBBONS wallhanging has Eight-Pointed Stars, Sawtooth Stars, and two blocks that are pieced Log Cabin style. Use foundation piecing for the Log Cabin and Ribbon blocks. You may want to make a sample Eight-Pointed Star before cutting your fabrics.

BLOCK ASSEMBLY

Eight-Pointed Stars:

★ Sew a 2⅛" red strip to a 2⅛" red-print strip, lengthwise with right sides together (a). Do not press open. Make a second set of strips like this.

★ Use the 45° angle of the rotary ruler to cut 20 2⅛" diagonal slices along the strips to make 20 pairs of diamonds (b). Set aside.

★ Cut five 4½" medium-gold squares diagonally twice like an X to make 20 base triangles for the Eight-Pointed Stars (c).

★ To sew a pair of red diamond star points to a base triangle, open the diamond pair (d). Match the tip of one red diamond with a 45° tip of the base triangle, right sides together.

★ Sew from the base to the top of the triangle. Stop. Align the second diamond with the other side of the triangle (e). Continue the seam to the base of the triangle. Sew the rest of the diamond pairs to the remaining base triangles.

★ Use four 2⅞" medium-gold squares for the corners of the star. Sew two of the star-point units to adjacent sides of a square to make half a star. Sew two additional star-point units to a second square to make the second half star (f).

a. sew strips together

b. cut diagonal slices along the strips

c. 4½" square, cut diagonally

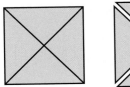

d. open diamond

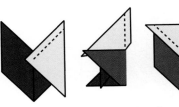

e. sew triangle to the diamonds, press seams

f. sew two-diamond units to a square

Fig. 6–10a–f. Eight-Pointed Star

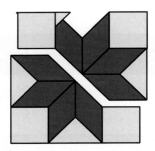

g. attach the corner squares to the star halves

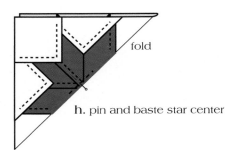

fold

h. pin and baste star center

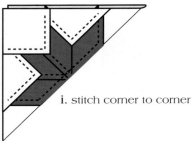

i. stitch corner to corner

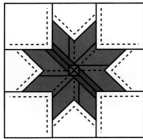

j. seam allowances will form a square in the center

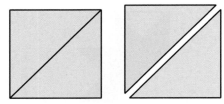

k. cut 7¼" square in half diagonally

Fig. 6–10h–l. Eight-Pointed Star, continued

★ Sew both halves of the star to a third square. Sew the opposite ends of the star halves to the fourth square (g).

★ Use one pin to match star-half center to star-half center. With four or five long stitches, baste across the center seams (h). Verify that the centers match before stitching the final seam. Sew from one corner to opposite corner (i).

★ From the wrong side, pick out the stitches that cross into the seam allowance so that the four seams can be pressed flat. The seam allowances will form a square at the center on the back (j). Make five Eight-Pointed stars.

★ The star at the center of the medallion is on point. To add the setting triangles, cut two medium-gold 7¼" squares in half diagonally (k). Mark the centers of the long sides of the four triangles and the sides of one of the star blocks.

★ Matching centers, sew the triangles to the sides of the star, overlapping the triangles at the corners of the star block. The 12½" center is now complete (l).

l. sew triangles to the sides of the star block

Giant Sawtooth Star

★ Place two 6½" teal-print squares face down on opposite ends of a 6½" x 12½" light-gold rectangle. Sew the diagonals of the squares to make the star-point units (Flying Geese) for the Giant Sawtooth Star (a). Cut away the waste triangles. Make four units.

★ Sew two completed star-point units to opposite sides of the Sawtooth Star's center square (b).

★ Sew a 6½" light-gold square to each end of the two remaining star-point units (c). Sew the star-point sections to the remaining sides of the center square to complete the Giant Sawtooth Star block for the center of the wall-hanging (d).

Star border: The first border contains eight accent blocks, four Eight-Pointed Stars (already made), and four Sawtooth Stars. The Sawtooth Stars are constructed like the Giant Sawtooth Star.

Sawtooth Stars

★ For the Sawtooth Star blocks, make 16 star-point units from the 2½" x 4½" medium-gold rectangles and the 2½" red-print squares.

★ Sew two star-point units to opposite sides of each of the four 4½" teal-print squares.

★ Sew a 2½" medium-gold square to each end of the remaining star-point units. Sew the star-point sections to the remaining sides of the center squares.

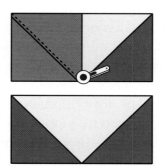

a. make the star-points units

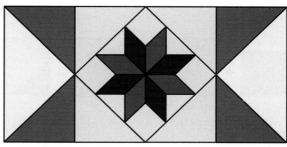

b. sew star-points units to opposite sides of center block

c. sew 6½" squares to two star-point units

d. sew star-point sections to the remaining sides

Fig. 6–11a–d. Giant Sawtooth Star

Accent blocks

★ Use the corner-square technique to add a teal corner (6½" squares) to eight 8½" medium-gold squares (a).

★ Sew two accent blocks to opposite sides of four Eight-Pointed Star blocks, with the upper teal corners pointing away from the star blocks, to make four border units (b).

★ Attach a border unit to opposite sides of the medallion center. Sew a Sawtooth Star on each end of the other two border units and sew these borders to the remaining sides of the medallion center (c).

Log Cabin border: The 20 Log Cabin blocks are foundation-pieced. The design is half of a Court House Steps block. Six blocks are sewn together for each side of the medallion. Each corner of the border ends with a star-point square.

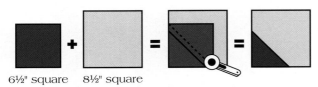

6½" square   8½" square

a. make the accent blocks using corner-square technique

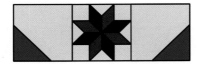

b. sew accent blocks to opposite sides of Eight-pointed Star blocks

c. sew border units to the medallion center

Fig. 6–12a–c. Accent Blocks

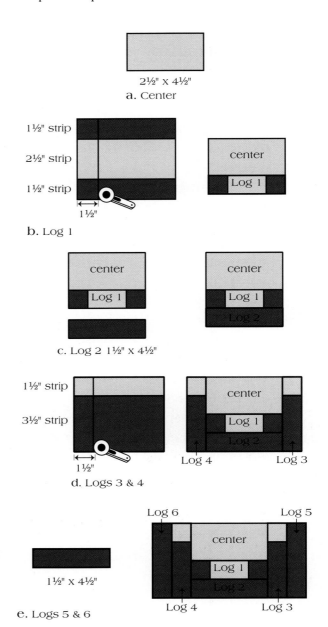

2½" x 4½"
a. Center

1½" strip
2½" strip
1½" strip
1½"

center
Log 1

b. Log 1

center
Log 1

center
Log 1
Log 2

c. Log 2 1½" x 4½"

1½" strip
3½" strip
1½"

center
Log 1
Log 2
Log 4   Log 3

d. Logs 3 & 4

Log 6   Log 5

center
Log 1
Log 2
Log 4   Log 3

1½" x 4½"

e. Logs 5 & 6

Fig. 6–13a–e. Log Cabin border half-blocks

★ Trace 20 Log Cabin half-blocks from the pattern on page 114. (Sheer, tear-away foundations are recommended.) Piece the logs by sewing fabric strips to the tear-away foundation in sequence.

CENTER

★ Pin a 2½" x 4½" medium-gold center rectangle to the foundation (Fig. 6–13a).

LOG 1

★ Sew a 2½" medium-gold strip between two 1½" teal-print strips to make a band of strips. Cut 20 1½" slices from the sewn strips. Sew the slices to the bottoms of each of the medium-gold centers (b).

LOG 2

★ Sew a 1½" x 4½" teal-print log 2 to the bottom of the first log for all the blocks (c).

LOGS 3 & 4

★ Make two sewn strips consisting of a 3½" teal-print strip and a 1½" medium-gold strip. Cut 40 1½" slices for logs 3 and 4. Sew the logs to the sides of the center section (d).

LOGS 5 & 6

★ Sew a 1½" x 4½" teal-print rectangle to each side of the center sections to complete the blocks (e).

LOG CABIN BORDER CORNERS

★ Fold the 2⅛" teal strip in half crosswise, right sides together. Stitch the strip halves along one edge (Fig. 6–14a). Cut four 2⅛"-wide pairs of teal star-points at a 45° angle from the doubled strip (b). Press the star-point pairs open.

★ Straddle one corner of each of the four 2⅞" teal-print squares with a star-point pair. Sew the star points to the square (c).

★ Cut the four 2⅛" teal-print squares in half diagonally to make eight half-square triangles (d). Sew triangles to the teal star points and trim the unit to 4½" x 4½" (includes seam allowances) (e).

a. fold and sew one edge of strip

b. cut diagonal slices along the strips

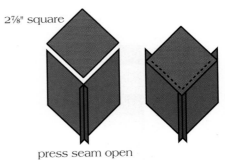

press seam open

c. sew the star point to the square

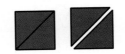

2⅛" square

d. cut square to make triangles

e. sew triangles to the star points

Fig. 6–14a–e. Log Cabin border corners

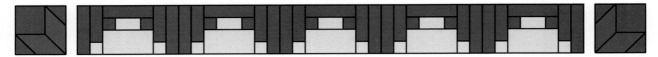

Fig. 6–15. Log Cabin border assembly

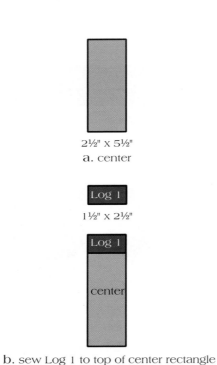

2½" x 5½"
a. center

Log 1

1½" x 2½"

b. sew Log 1 to top of center rectangle

1½" square   1½" x 6½"   1½" square

c. use the corner-square technique to sew squares on both ends of the rectangle

Fig. 6–16a–c. Ribbon Border Blocks

BORDER ASSEMBLY

★ Sew five Log Cabin blocks together for each side of the quilt.

★ Sew teal star-point corners to the ends of two of the Log Cabin borders. Sew the Log Cabin borders as shown in the border assembly diagram (Fig. 6–15).

Ribbon border

★ The 32 Ribbon blocks finish 6" x 6" and are foundation pieced (pattern on page 115). There are eight blocks on each side of the quilt, and a 1½" dark-gold strip runs across the top and bottom of the blocks. The ribbon continues through the 8" Sawtooth Stars in each corner.

RIBBON BLOCKS

★ Trace the pattern, page 115, on 32 sheer, tear-away foundations. The logs are cut from individual strips of fabric or from two or more strips sewn together. Additionally, logs 5 and 6 have triangles at each end, sewn with the corner-square technique. Piece the logs to the foundations in sequence.

CENTER

★ Pin or lightly paste the 2½" x 5½" dark-gold center rectangles to the foundations (a).

LOG 1

★ Sew the 1½" x 2½" red rectangles to the tops of the center rectangles (b).

Logs 2 & 3

★ Use the corner-square technique to add dark-gold triangles to red-print rectangles, as follows:

★ Place a 1½" dark-gold square at each end of 32 of the 1½" x 6½" red-print rectangles. Sew the diagonals of the squares from the lower-left to the upper-right (c). (The diagonal seams will be parallel to each other.)

★ For the remaining 32 logs, sew the squares on the opposite diagonal (d). Cut away the outer waste triangles. Sew logs 2 and 3 to the sides of the center section (e).

Logs 4 & 5

★ Use the 5½" dark-gold strips and the 1½" red strips to make three sewn strips. Cut 64 1½" slices from the sewn strips and sew them to the blocks (f).

Border assembly

★ Sew eight Ribbon blocks together for each side of the wallhanging.

★ For the dark-gold strips along the top and bottom of the Ribbon blocks, use bias seams to join the ten 1½" dark-gold strips, end to end, as needed to make eight 1½" x 48½" strips. Sew the strips to the top and bottom of each of the four ribbon-border rows (Fig. 6–17)). Sew the borders to the quilt as shown in the ribbon border assembly diagram.

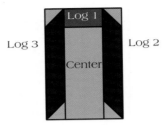

d. sew square on the logs in the opposite direction

e. sew logs 2 and 3 to the center section

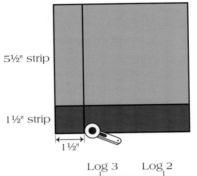

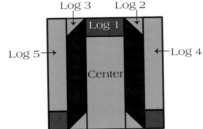

f. sew logs 4 and 5 to the center section

Fig. 6–16d–f. Ribbon Border Blocks, continued

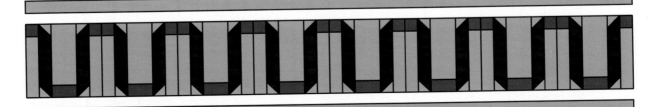

Fig. 6–17. Ribbon border assembly

Log Cabin Border Half-Blocks

Use this pattern to trace foundations for 20 Log Cabin half-blocks. Instructions are on pages 110–111.

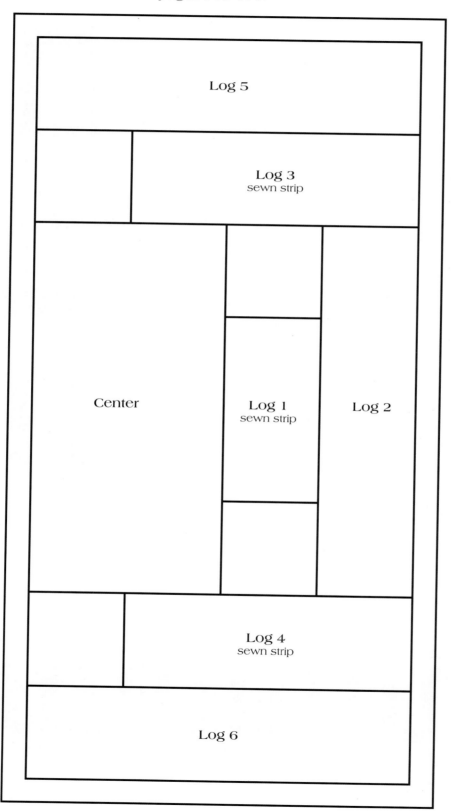

Ribbon Border Block

Use this pattern to trace 32 Ribbon Blocks. Instructions are on pages 112–113.

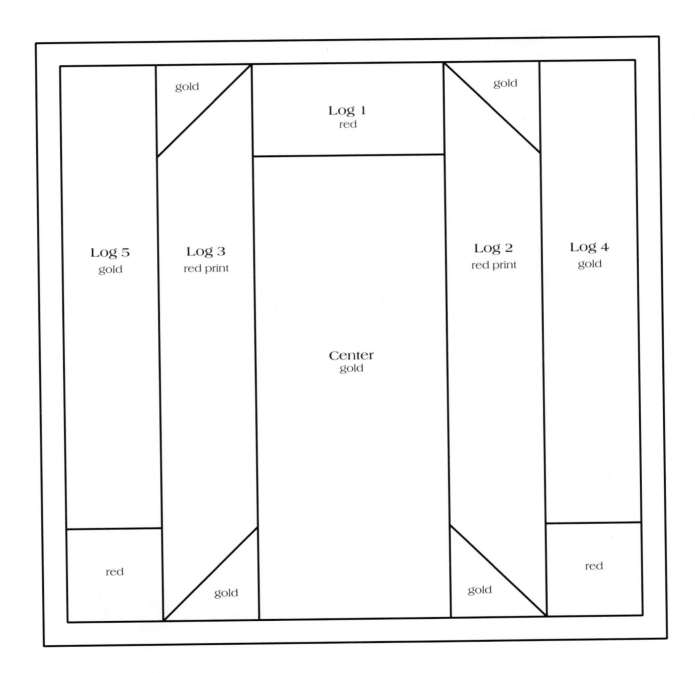

1⅞" square

a. make half-squares

1½" x 2½"

b. sew half-squares to rectangle

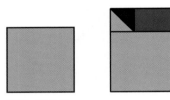

3½" square

c. sew the rectangle unit to square

1½" square   4½" x 1½"   1½" square

d. use the corner-square technique to sew squares on rectangle

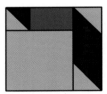

e. sew the rectangle unit to the center section

1½" square   half-square

f. make ribbon fragment blocks for two corners

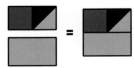

1½" x 2½"

g. sew ribbon fragment unit to rectangle

Fig. 6–17a–h. Star corner blocks

STAR CORNER BLOCKS

★ Use six 1⅞" dark-gold and six 1⅞" red-print squares to make twelve 1½" half-squares (Fig. 6–17a). Sew a half-square to one end of each of the four red 1½" x 2½" rectangles (b). Set the remaining half-squares aside. Sew the rectangle units to the four 3½" dark-gold squares (c).

★ Lay the four 1½" x 4½" red-print rectangles in a horizontal position. Place a 1½" dark-gold square at each end of the four strips. Sew the diagonal of the squares as shown in (d). Cut away the waste triangles. Sew the rectangle units to the center section.

★ Two of the 2½" squares in the corners of the star blocks are plain dark gold. Two of the squares have ribbon fragments.

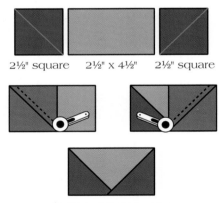

2½" square   2½" x 4½"   2½" square

h. Flying Geese units

i. Finished star corner block

★ To make the ones with ribbon fragments, sew a 1½" red square to
the red-print end of the eight
remaining half-squares (f).

★ Sew one of these units to each of
the eight dark-gold 1½" x 2½" rectangles to complete the ribbon-
fragment corner-squares (g).

★ For the 16 Flying Geese units for
the star points, use the corner-
square technique to sew the 2½"
teal-print squares to the 2½" x 4½"
dark-gold rectangles (h).

★ For assembly, arrange the pieces
of the block and two 2½" dark-gold
squares on a flat surface. Position
the ribbon fragments in the corners to suggest the continuation of

the ribbon from one side of the
wall hanging to the next. Sew the
pieces together to complete the
Sawtooth Star block. Make four
blocks.

★ Sew a Sawtooth Star block to each
end of two Ribbon strips. Sew a
strip of eight Ribbon blocks to two
sides of the wallhanging followed
by Ribbon strips with the Sawtooth
star blocks at the ends to complete
the final border (Fig. 6–18).

FINISHING

Layer the quilt with batting and a backing,
then quilt the layers. Bind the raw edges of
the quilt with 2" continuous, double-fold bias
binding.

Fig. 6–18. Quilt assembly

Fig. 6–19. Completed quilt top

Chapter 7

Strip-Pieced Diamond Stars

The strip-piecing technique is among the earliest speed methods learned for machine-sewn quilts. It is obvious that patterns as simple as a four-patch block can be quickly pieced by sewing two strips at a time. Like making squares for the four-patch, it is faster, easier, and more accurate to sew strips together to make diamonds and parallelograms for stars. In strip piecing these shapes, the fabric is cut on the straight of grain, the sewn strips are sliced on the bias, and the bias slices are sewn to another piece with straight edges to stabilize the bias-cut unit.

a. Northumberland Star

b. Union Star

c. Liberty Star

d. Dove in the Window

Fig. 7–1a–d. Blocks using strip-pieced diamonds or parallelograms.

Fig. 7–2. Lone Star

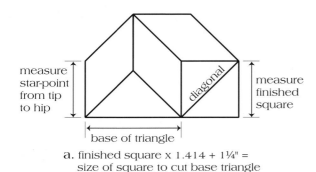

a. finished square x 1.414 + 1¼" = size of square to cut base triangle

Fig. 7–3a. Base triangles for Lone Star blocks

Star points can be diamond or parallelogram shaped. Parallelograms, like diamonds, have two parallel sets of sides, but their sides are not equal in length, and the widths between the parallel sides are not equal. Like diamonds, parallelograms can be sewn and cut by using strip piecing.

When multiple fabric strips are sewn together into layers and then cut, several equal-sized sets of diamonds or parallelograms are produced. By planning the layering of the strata by the number of strips, strip width, and color, different designs can be made.

Examples of strip piecing to make diamond or parallelogram star-points include the Northumberland Star (diamonds) (Fig. 7–1a) and the Union Star (parallelograms) (b). Layered strips can be sewn to make patterns within individual diamonds, such as the three-stripe Liberty Star (c). Strata can also be sewn to make figurative patterns like Dove in the Window (d).

The Lone Star, like the Eight-Pointed Star block, is an octagon-based star. It is sewn using multiples of 45° diamonds rather than 8 individual diamonds. Lone Stars are sewn using the strip method to create rows of stars.

The size of the Lone Star may be designed to fit within 54", 60", or 76" squares, the largest squares that fit the double, queen, or king mattress tops. A common means of enlarging the Lone Star, however, is to add an additional row to the star-point changing a 5 diamond/5 row star-point into a 6 diamond/6 row star-point. For example, when using a 2" diamond, the increase of one diamond enlarges the Lone Star by 5¾".

Differences in quilt sizes also depend on the design. The Lone Star set within a square with four squares and four base triangles between star-points is much smaller than the same Lone Star in a Rolling Star setting when the eight squares between star-points are incorporated into the design.

To design a Lone Star (Fig. 7–2), determine (1) the size of the individual diamonds, (2) the number of rows within the eight star-points, and (3) the size of the squares between the star-points, or if the Lone Star is to be made into a rectangular shape, the size of the base triangles between four of the star-points.

The size of the setting squares between the star-points can be determined after the whole star has been sewn unless the squares are design blocks. Measure a finished diamond row inside a star-point as the outer edges may have been stretched.

When the Lone Star is used with four squares and four base triangles, the long side of the base triangle is equal to the diagonal of the corner square (Fig. 7–3). To find the diagonal, multiply the measurement of the setting square by 1.414. Add 1¼" for seam allowances to determine the size of square to cut to make the base triangle (a). Cut the square diagonally twice like an X (b).

MEASURING THE DIAMOND

Diamond measurements are described by degree and width. To measure the size of the Lone Star, the length of the sides must also be measured: 1½" width = length of side of 2⅛"; 2" width = length of side of 2⅞"; 2½" width = length of side of 3½"; and 3" width = length of side of 4¼". (Fig. 7–4).

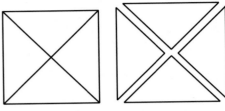

b. make diagonal cuts

Fig. 7–3b. Base triangles for Lone Star blocks

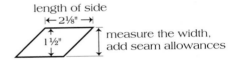

length of side
|← 2⅛" →|
1½"
measure the width, add seam allowances

Fig. 7–4. Determine width of strips

Make a Lone Star without a pattern

★ ★ ★

★ Select a diamond size such as the 2" diamond.

★ Measure the sides of the diamond (2⅞") or 2.875")

★ Decide the star-points may have 5 or 6 rows of stars.

★ Multiply 2.875" x 5 = 14.375" which is the size of the corner square (sides of diamonds x number of rows).

★ The base triangle is 1.414 x the corner square. Multiply 14.375" x 1.414 = 20.326".

★ Add two corners plus one base triangle to find the size of the square that will encompass the Lone Star. Add 14.375" + 20.326" = 14.375" = 49.076" or a 49" square.

★ Cut 2½" strips of fabric for the strata that will finish as 2" diamonds.

★ Cut 45°, 2½" wide slices from the 5 layer strata.

★ Lay out 5 45° slices for each star-point.

★ Sew the slices into star-point pairs, then quarters, then halves and finally the whole.

★ Measure a star-point from tip to hip to find the size of the corner square. Multiply the side of the corner square by 1.414 to find the size of the base triangle and add 1¼" to the result. Cut the square diagonally twice.

★ Set in the corners and base triangles. Add borders to make a double comforter that measures 76" x 86".

VICTORIAN MIDNIGHT, 120" x 120", made by Edna Gregory. The diamond is cut as 3", which is 2½" finished. The six rows include black,
pale rose, light rose, medium rose, dark rose, and the rose figure
on a white background.

VICTORIAN MIDNIGHT, shown on page 122, is a Lone Star set to resemble the Rolling Star block (Fig. 7–5). The design of the star is a modified repeat, created with the use of both the strip-piecing technique and individual piecing of the center star.

The quilt utilizes coordinating fabric in the blocks and border prints. To adapt the size of the pre-printed fabric blocks to the size needed for the quilt, the blocks were enlarged by bordering them with strips, which were pieced Log Cabin style. To make the rose wreath at the center, the rose design was traced on template material to aid in cutting identical rose diamonds.

The star "floats" within the bordered edge because of the "logs" that surround the pre-printed blocks between the star points. To "square" the octagon formed by the star, a square and triangular half were sewn first to the right and then to the left of the center pre-printed squares that lie on point at the top and bottom of the quilt. Two additional square and triangular halves complete each side.

This "squaring" of the points of the octagon shape continue the Log Cabin style used in enlarging the pre-printed blocks. A single wedge is a second means of squaring the octagon. The wedge shape automatically "miters" at the corner.

The Lone Star as depicted by VICTORIAN MIDNIGHT is an example of contemporary Lone Stars whose star points commonly have four to six divisions. It is also an example of the rolling-star setting. Another Lone Star setting is the Broken Star, which is the Carpenter's Wheel design (Fig. 7–6).

Additionally, small Lone Stars can be sewn in an overall set that resembles lattice when small stars touch point to point across the quilt horizontally and vertically (Fig. 7–7).

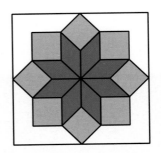

Fig. 7–5. Rolling Star block

Fig. 7–6. Carpenter's Wheel setting

Fig. 7–7. Lone Star in overall set

CHINOOK, 61" x 61", designed and pieced by the author and quilted by Vi Russell.

CHINOOK
61" x 61"

1 Lone Star
8 Chinook blocks, 10⅝"

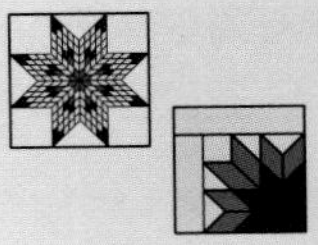

★ ★ ★
**strip-pieced
Lone Star**
p. 126

Cut strips selvage to selvage. Be sure to label all your pieces with their cut sizes.

Materials	Yds.	First cut		Second cut	
Lt. Gray	2				
Lone Star		18 strips	2"	strip piecing	
Chinook blocks		1 strip	5½"	4 squares	5½"
		1 strip	3"	8 squares	3"
		1 strip	2⅝"	8 squares	2⅝"
		2 strips	2⅝"	8 rectangles	2⅝" x 9"
		3 strips	2⅝"	8 rectangles	2⅝" x 11⅛"
Black	2½				
Lone Star		5 strips	2"	strip piecing	
(background)		1 piece	36" x 65"	(see wedges, page 130)	
Chinook blocks		2 strips	2"	strip piecing	
		1 strip	5⅛"	4 squares	5⅛"
Red	1¾				
Lone Star		2 strips	2"	strip piecing	
Chinook blocks		4 strips	2"	strip piecing	
Border		6 strips	4½"	strip piecing	
Binding		1 rectangle	18" x 42"		
Border print	½	6 strips	1½"		
Backing	3⅝	2 panels	33" x 65"		
Batting		65" x 65"			

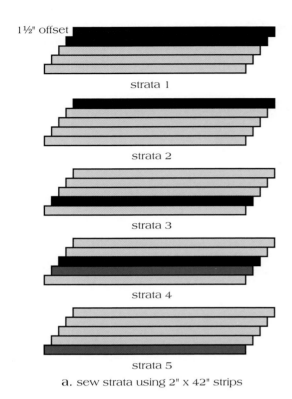

strata 1

strata 2

strata 3

strata 4

strata 5

a. sew strata using 2" x 42" strips

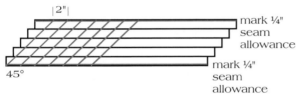

b. trim and cut slices

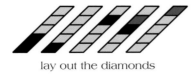

lay out the diamonds

sew diamonds

c. lay out and sew diamonds

Fig. 7–8a–c. Lone Star

Sewing

Block assembly

It is important to cut, sew, and press carefully when working with diamonds because of the bias edges. It is also important that the small diamonds and the large diamond star points are the correct measurements before the star is assembled so the Chinook blocks and black background pieces will fit the star.

Each layer in the 5" layer strata must measure 1½" finished.

Lone Star

Note that, for the small diamonds, each of the five different strip combinations (strata sets) contains five 2" strips. To maximize the number of diamonds you can cut from a strata set, off-set each strip 1½", forming a stair-stepped 45° angle. Make the five strata sets as shown in Fig. 7–8a.

★ Trim off the stair steps to make a 45° beginning cut. Mark ¼" seam allowances along the top and bottom diamonds in each row. Cut eight 2"-wide 45° slices from each of the five strata sets (b).

★ Arrange the five 45° slices into eight identical large diamonds with each diamond having five rows of small diamonds (c).

★ Place the slices right sides together and match the individual seams of each of the diamonds. Sew the five slices together in order (c). Press carefully.

★ To assemble the star points, place two large diamonds right sides together. Sew the large diamonds into pairs (d). Place two pairs right sides together and sew the pairs into halves (e).

★ Match the centers of the two halves and pin. Baste the seam intersections at the center (f). Open the halves to verify that the center seams match. Proceed to sew the halves into one whole star (g).

d. sew two diamonds together

f. pin and baste half stars

e. sew the pairs into half stars

g. sew the halves

h. whole star

Fig. 7–8d–h. Lone Star, continued

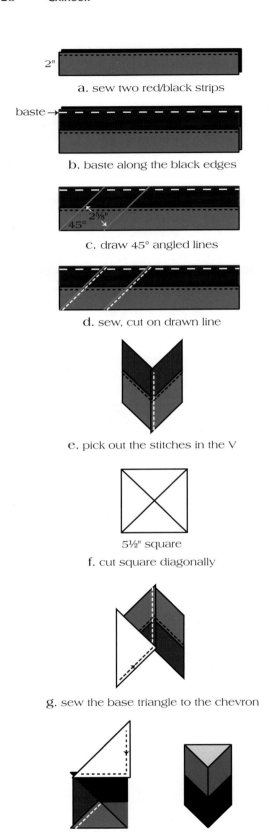

2"

a. sew two red/black strips

baste →

b. baste along the black edges

2⅝"
45°

c. draw 45° angled lines

d. sew, cut on drawn line

e. pick out the stitches in the V

5½" square

f. cut square diagonally

g. sew the base triangle to the chevron

h. sew the base triangle to the chevron

Fig. 7–9a–h. Chevron units

Chinook blocks

The Chinook blocks that lie between the star points finish 10⅝".

CHEVRON UNITS

★ Sew a 2" black strip and a 2" red strip together lengthwise (Fig. 7–9a). Make two black/red pairs of strips. Press the seam allowance of one pair toward the black strip. Press the seam allowance of the second pair toward the red strip.

★ With right sides together, machine baste the edges of each pair of black/red strips along the black edges (b). Press. (Do not press open.)

★ Draw – do not cut – 45° parallel lines every 2⅝" across the strips (c). With a ¼" seam allowance, sew across the strips to the right of each drawn line (d). Cut on the drawn lines. Cut a total of 16 units.

★ Pick out the row of basting stitches at the top of the black strips. Open the double-V chevrons. Pick out the stitches in the seam allowance at the inside point of the V (e).

★ Cut the four 5½" gray squares into quarters diagonally to use as base triangles (f). With right sides together, match and sew the black/red chevrons to the 16 gray base triangles, as follows:

★ Match the legs of the chevrons to the 45° angles of the base triangles as shown in (g). Stitch from the bottom of the triangle to the peak. Match and stitch the second leg to the adjacent side of the base triangle (h). Sew all 16 units. Set the chevron units aside.

PARALLELOGRAM UNITS

★ Sew two 2" red strips together lengthwise (7–10a). Do not press open. Cut eight 2⅝" 45° slices from the layered red strips (b). Press the parallelogram pairs open.

★ Straddle the corner of each of the 16 2⅝" gray squares with a pair of red parallelograms (c). Stitch in place with a ¼" seam allowance.

★ Cut the eight 3" gray squares in half diagonally (d). Stitch a triangle to each side of the parallelogram pairs to make a 4¾" square (e).

★ Sew a chevron unit to each side of a parallelogram unit (f). Sew the two chevron units together like mitering a corner.

★ Cut the four 5⅛" black squares in half diagonally to make eight triangles (g). Sew a triangle to the chevron side of each block. Press and trim the blocks to 9" (unfinished).

★ Sew a 2⅝" x 9" gray rectangle to the left edge of each Chinook block. Sew the remaining 2⅝" x 11⅛" rectangles as shown in the block assembly (Fig. 7–11) to complete the Chinook block. Make eight blocks.

3" square

d. cut squares diagonally

e. stitch triangles to sides of parallelogram pairs

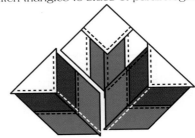

f. sew a chevron unit to each side of parallelogram unit

5⅛" square

g. cut square diagonally

Fig. 7–10d–g. Parallelogram units

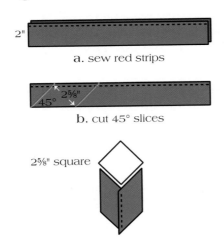

2"

a. sew red strips

2⅝"

45°

b. cut 45° slices

2⅝" square

c. sew parallelogram pair to square

Fig. 7–10a–c. Parallelogram units

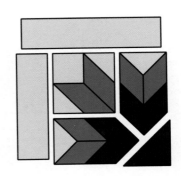

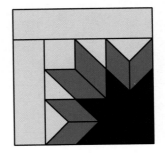

Fig. 7–11. Block assembly

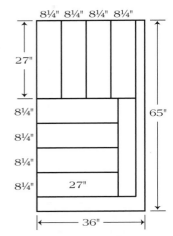

8¼" 8¼" 8¼" 8¼"

27"

8¼"

8¼"

8¼"

8¼"

65"

27"

36"

a. wedge cutting diagram

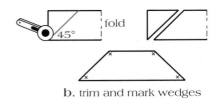

45°   fold

b. trim and mark wedges

c. sew the wedge to the top of square

Fig. 7–12a–c. Wedges

QUILT ASSEMBLY

★ Sew the eight 11⅛" (unfinished) Chinook blocks between the star points, as shown in Fig. 7–13, in the following manner: Sew from the bottom of the inside V to the marked seam allowance at the tip of the large diamond. Repeat for the other side of the block. Sew all eight Chinook blocks to the star. Press the seam allowances toward the blocks.

Wedges

Use the following directions to cut the black background wedges to keep the grain of the fabric the same in all the wedges. Mark each wedge as horizontal or vertical on the wrong side of the fabric as each rectangle is cut.

★ To cut the wedges from the black 36" x 65" (slightly oversized) piece, first cut a 27"-length of the fabric, as shown in the wedge cutting diagram. Cut this strip into four vertical 8¼" x 27" pieces. Cut a 27"-wide strip parallel to the selvages. Cut this strip into four horizontal 8¼" x 27" pieces (Fig. 7–12a).

★ Fold the eight rectangles in half, matching the short ends. Cut away a 45° triangle from the end of each folded rectangle. The wedges that remain include seam allowances (b).

★ Mark the seam allowance intersections at each corner of the eight wedges. Sew the tops of the wedges to the Chinook blocks that point to the corners of the quilt (c). (Do not sew into the seam allowances.) Next, sew one angled side of each wedge to the adjacent Chinook block on point (d). Continue sewing the horizontal and vertical wedges to the Chinook block. Finally, miter the wedges together at the corners (e).

★ For the red border, use a bias seam to sew the six 4½" strips, end to end, to make the lengths needed for the quilt. Sew the 1½" print border strips together and cut to size.

★ Sew a red border strip to a print border strip lengthwise. Repeat for the other border strips. Treat the combined strips as one. Sew the borders to the quilt with the print border on the outside and miter the corners.

FINISHING

Layer the quilt with batting and a backing, then quilt the layers. Bind the raw edges of the quilt with 2" continuous, double-fold bias binding.

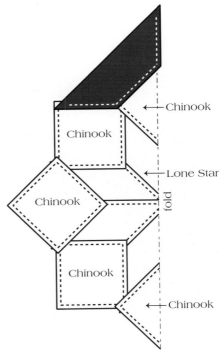

e. miter the wedges at the corner

Fig. 7–12e. Wedges

d. stitch one angled end to the block on point

Fig. 7–12d. Wedges

Fig. 7–13. Quilt assembly

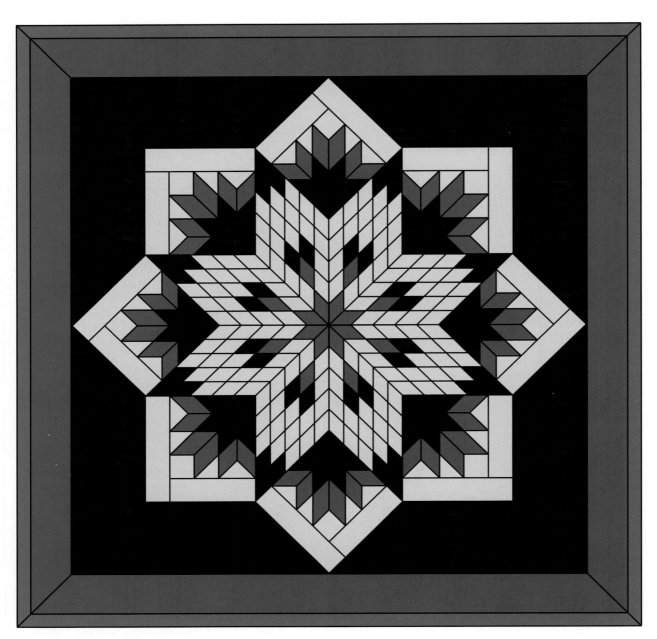

Fig. 7–14. Completed quilt top

Chapter 8

Log Cabin Stars

The Log Cabin techniques of sewing strips (logs) in clockwise or counterclockwise sequence, or by alternating from side to side/top to bottom, can be used to make star-point units or blocks like Delectable Mountain.

The two most common Log Cabin block designs, Log Cabin and Courthouse Steps, both have a central square, which can vary in size. In the traditional Log Cabin (Fig. 8–1a), rectangular strips are added in a clockwise or counter-clockwise direction. Each strip overlaps the last applied strip. In Courthouse Steps, the strips are added in the sequence of top, bottom, side, side, etc. (b).

Both Log Cabin block designs begin with a square and finish as a square. When the technique of sewing strips (logs) to a central geometric figure other than a square is used, more design possibilities can occur. The term "Log Cabin," as used here, refers to the construction technique rather than the block design itself.

When the Log Cabin technique is used to sew 45° or 60° diamonds, a Log Cabin star can be produced. Large over-all designs like the Lone Star can be made with Log Cabin diamonds. The color and design variations are determined according to the values and arrangements of the logs within the diamonds.

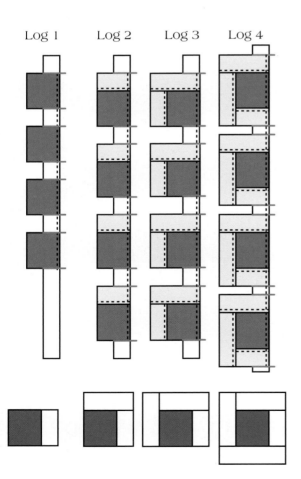

Fig. 8–1a. Traditional Log Cabin

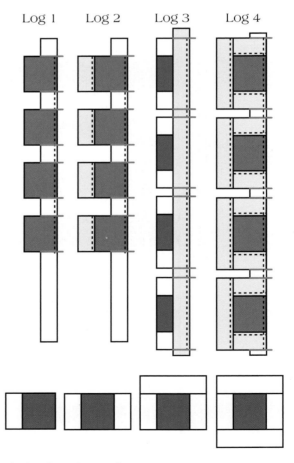

Fig. 8–1b. Courthouse Steps

The star as a design component of the Log Cabin block is illustrated in the LOG CABIN STAR quilt, page 139. The quilt design includes the classic Aunt Eliza's Star, which is sewn Log Cabin-style (Fig. 8–2). The Aunt Eliza's Star is then set within the traditional Log Cabin block, which was cut diagonally and re-sewn to produce the new four-block star.

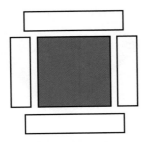

a. chain piece the logs to the center square

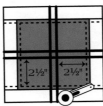

b. cut the block into quarters, 2¼" from seam line

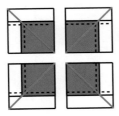

c. draw lines from the corners to the center

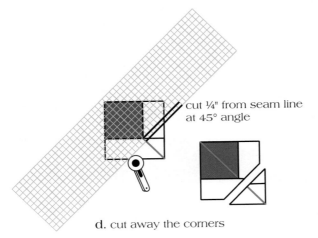

cut ¼" from seam line at 45° angle

d. cut away the corners

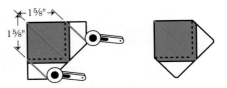

e. trim the corners 1⅝" from drawn line to make star-point units

3¼" square

f. cut squares twice on the diagonal

g. sew triangles to sides of the star-point units

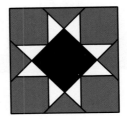

3¼" square

h. block assembly

Fig. 8–2a–h. Aunt Eliza's Star block

LEWIS AND CLARK, 65" x 75", made by Shirley Anderson, uses the Log Cabin Pineapple technique to make Delectable Mountain blocks and the half-square technique to make Delectable Mountain borders in strips.

The LEWIS AND CLARK quilt was designed as a foundation-pieced Log Cabin for the traditional Delectable Mountains block. The traditional Log Cabin Pineapple was re-cut to produce the Delectable Mountains block (Fig. 8–3). A second technique for Delectable Mountains uses half-squares for the quilt border (Fig. 8–5, page 138). Delectable Mountains appears as a strip design in the early quilt design books.

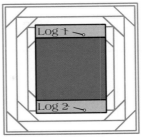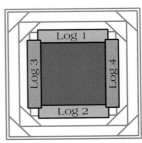

e. stitch Log 2 to opposite side; sew Logs 3 and 4

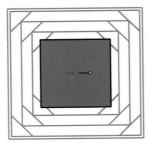

a. pin square to foundation

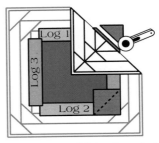

f. place a square even with the edges of the logs

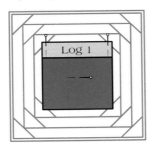

b. align Log 1 with edge of center square

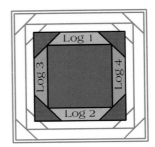

g. turn to the right side, fold the foundation away
   from the sewn corner. Trim the square and logs.

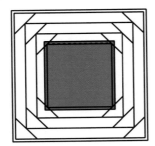

c. turn foundation over, sew on line

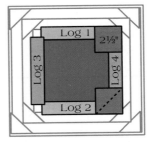

h. sew all four corners, before adding
   next round of logs

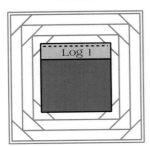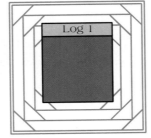

d. turn block to right side, finger press Log 1

Fig. 8–3. Delectable Mountain block

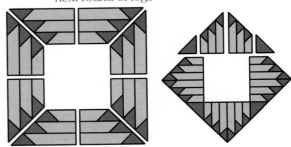

i. Cut block horizontally, vertically, and on both diagonals

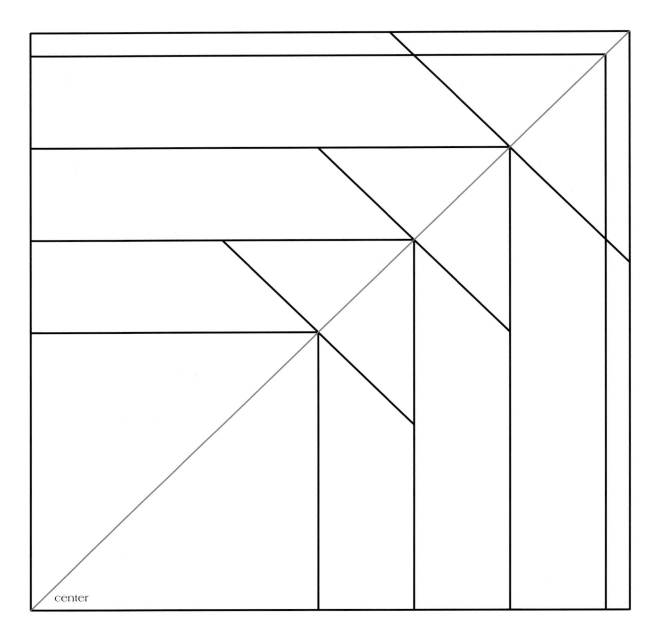

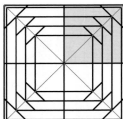

Fig. 8–4. Full-size foundation for ¼ Log Cabin block for the Delectable Mountain block.

  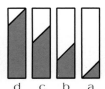

a b c d   d c b a

Fig. 8–5. Delectable Mountain border uses half-squares.

LOG CABIN STAR

LOG CABIN STAR, 90" x 106½", made by Lella King and quilted by Gloria Badgett.

LOG CABIN STAR
90" x 106½"

36 Log Cabin Stars, 15¼"

★ ★ ★

Log Cabin star points
p. 143

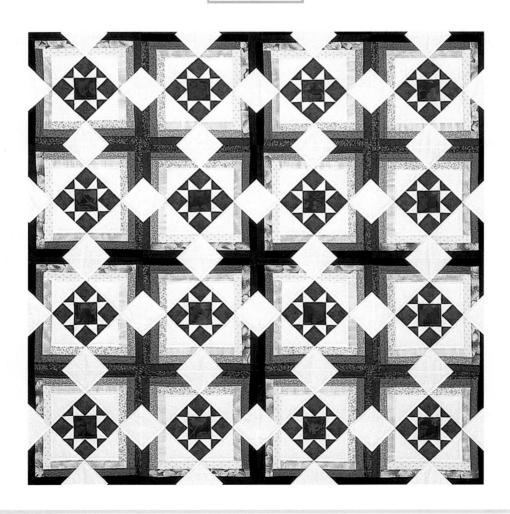

Cut strips selvage to selvage. Be sure to label all your pieces with their cut sizes.

Materials	Yds.	First cut		Second cut	
White	2¾				
Log Cabin Star					
centers		4 strips	9¾"	36 squares	9¾"
base triangles		5 strips	7¼"	30 squares	7¼"
Aunt Eliza's Stars					
star-point units		7 strips	1½"	132 rectangles	1½" x 5½"
star-point units		5 strips	1½"	132 rectangles	1½" x 7½"
Dark teal	2¼				
Log Cabin Star					
base triangles		5 strips	7¼"	6 squares	7¼"
Border strips		14 strips	2¾"		
Log Cabin logs					
Light					
log 1	½	9 strips	1½"	36 rectangles	1½" x 9¾"
log 2	½	12 strips	1½"	36 rectangles	1½" x 10¾"
log 3	½	12 strips	1½"	36 rectangles	1½" x 10¾"
log 4	½	12 strips	1½"	36 rectangles	1½" x 11¾"
Medium					
log 5	⅝	12 strips	1½"	36 rectangles	1½" x 11¾"
log 6	⅝	12 strips	1½"	36 rectangles	1½" x 12¾"
log 7	⅝	12 strips	1½"	36 rectangles	1½" x 12¾"
log 8	⅝	12 strips	1½"	36 rectangles	1½" x 13¾"
Dark					
log 9	⅝	12 strips	1½"	36 rectangles	1½" x 13¾"
log 10	⅞	18 strips	1½"	36 rectangles	1½" x 14¾"
log 11	⅞	18 strips	1½"	36 rectangles	1½" x 14¾"
log 12	¾	18 strips	1½"	36 rectangles	1½" x 15¾"
Teal	2¼				
Aunt Eliza's Stars					
star-point units		10 strips	5½"	66 squares	5½"
base triangles		6 strips	3¼"	66 squares	3¼"
Blue green	⅝				
Aunt Eliza's Stars					
centers		6 strips	3½"	66 squares	(use template)
Backing	8	3 panels	37½" x 94"		
Binding	½				
Batting		94" x 110½"			

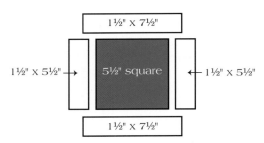

a. chain piece logs to the center square

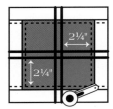

b. cut block into quarters, 2¼" from seam line

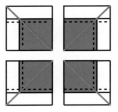

c. draw lines from the corners to the center

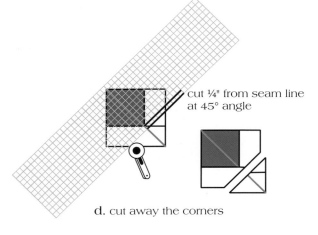

d. cut away the corners

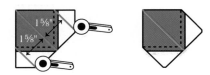

e. trim the corners 1⅝" from drawn line
   to make star-point units

Fig. 8–6a–e. Aunt Eliza's Star block

Sewing

BLOCK ASSEMBLY

Aunt Eliza's Star

The star-point units for the Aunt Eliza's Star blocks begin as Courthouse Steps blocks with only one log on each side.

★ Chain-piece the 1½" x 5½" white logs to opposite sides of the 5½" teal squares (Fig. 8–6a). Sew the 1½" x 7½" logs to the remaining sides of the squares to complete the 66 blocks.

★ Turn the bordered squares to the wrong side. Place the 2¼" line of the ruler on one seam line that joins a log to the square. Cut across the square. Repeat this cut on all four sides to quarter the block (b). Scraps between the quarters will remain after cutting. Draw lines on the wrong side from the corners to the center (c).

★ Where the logs overlap, cut off the corners of the units, leaving a ¼" seam allowance beyond the teal point, as follows: Align the 45° line of the rotary ruler with the seam line. Position the cutting edge ¼" from the corner of the teal square to allow for the seam allowance. Cut away the corner (d).

★ Next, cut away the corners adjacent to the just cut edge, as follows: On the back of the unit, measure 1⅝" from the drawn mid line as shown in (e). Cut off one side of the unit. Repeat for the other side. Cut all the star-point units this way.

★ Cut 66 teal 3¼" squares twice on the diagonal, like an X, to make the base triangles for the Aunt Eliza's Stars (f).

★ For each star, sew star-point units

to opposite sides of the 3¼" blue-green center squares as shown in the Block assembly, page 144.

★ Sew a base triangle to both sides of two other units (g). Sew these to the two remaining sides of the center square to complete the star.

Log Cabin Stars

The Log Cabin star-point units are made from Log Cabin blocks cut in quarters.

★ Use Log Cabin piecing in a clockwise direction to chain piece the logs to 36 9¾" white squares (Fig. 8–7a). The squares will have three logs on each side when complete.

★ Spray the Log Cabin blocks with fabric sizing to avoid stretching the bias cut edges created in the next steps.

★ On the wrong side of the 15¼" unfinished blocks, draw a 6½" wide X from corner to corner, as follows: Center the 3¼" line of the ruler on one diagonal pair of corners. Draw a line. Then rotate the square to measure and draw the opposite side of the 6½"-wide diagonal (b). Draw the second 6½"-wide diagonal to complete the X.

★ Cut the 6½"-wide X from the Log Cabin leaving a 6½" square on point and four base triangles as scrap (c, page 144).

★ Cut the 7¼" white squares and the 7¼" dark teal squares twice diagonally to make new base triangles for the Log Cabin Star blocks (d, page 144).

★ Lay out each unit of the block. Replace the original white square on point with an on-point Aunt Eliza's Star. Replace the Log Cabin's base triangles with two white and/or

3¼" square

f. cut squares twice on the diagonal

g. sew triangles to sides of the star-point units

3¼" square

h. Block assembly

Fig. 8–6f–h. Aunt Eliza's Star block, continued

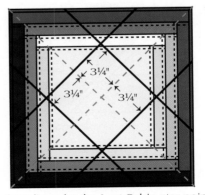

a. piece Log Cabin block

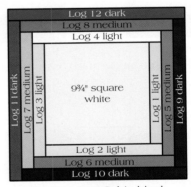

b. draw lines for the Log Cabin star points

Fig. 8–7a–b. Log Cabin Star points

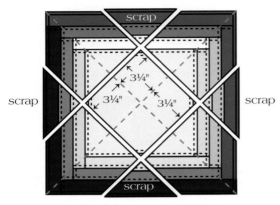

c. cut on the drawn lines

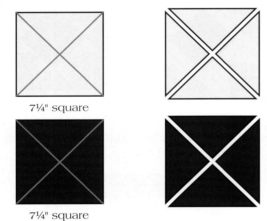

7¼" square

7¼" square

d. cut squares to make base triangles

Block assembly

Fig. 8–7c–d. Log Cabin Stars, continued

dark teal triangles. (The blocks at the edges of the quilt will have one dark teal base triangles or two dark teal triangles if the block is a corner block.)

★ Sew two Log Cabin star-point units to opposite sides of the new Aunt's Eliza's Star center as shown in the Block assembly.

★ Sew two white and/or teal base triangles to each side of two Log Cabin units. Sew these units to the block. Make 36 Log Cabin Star blocks.

QUILT ASSEMBLY

★ Sew the star blocks into four-block units (Fig. 8–8). Sew three of the four-block units across and three down to make the quilt body.

★ Use bias seams to sew the 2¾" dark teal border strips, end to end, as needed to make two 92" lengths and four 96½" lengths.

★ Sew a 96½" dark teal border strip to each side of the quilt body. Sew two 96½" strips to the top and bottom of the quilt.

★ Sew the remaining 30 Aunt Eliza's Stars into two rows of 15 stars for the borders at the top and at the bottom of the quilt. Sew the star borders to the quilt.

★ Sew a 96½" dark teal strip to the top and bottom to complete the quilt top.

FINISHING

Layer the quilt with batting and a backing, then quilt the layers. Bind the raw edges of the quilt with 2" continuous, double-fold bias binding.

Fig. 8–8. Quilt assembly

Fig. 8–9. Completed quilt top

Chapter 9

Feathered Stars

Feathered stars are basic star designs with feathers added to embellish their simple design lines. Try "fuss-free-feathers" for the octagon star.

Fig. 9–1. Octagon Star

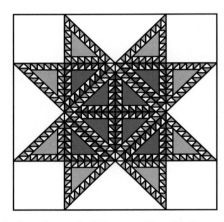

Fig. 9–2. Star Spangled Banner Star, feathers inside the four-patch (Sawtooth)

Fig. 9–3. Feathered Star, feathers in 2 sizes outside the Ohio Star on point.

Feathered Stars can be recognized as basic stars that have been outlined with half squares. The number of feathers on each side of a star point will be equal in number if the star is based on a perfect geometric figure such as the pentagon or hexagon (Fig. 9–1). (The star points of an octagon star have sides equal in length and therefore the same number of feathers on both sides.) Some octagon stars have two feathers and some have three. Feathers can also embellish the four-patch (Fig. 9–2) and Ohio Star blocks (Fig. 9–3).

FUSS-FREE FEATHERS FOR THE OCTAGON STAR

★ Draw a 45° diamond smaller than the diamond needed that is easily divided into smaller diamonds (9–5a). For example a 1½" 45° diamond divides into ½" diamonds.

★ Divide the diamond into smaller equal diamonds (b).

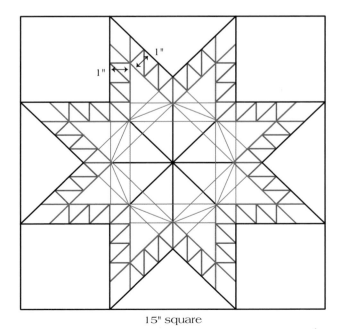

15" square

Fig. 9–4. Drawing the Feathered Star

★ Draw right angle lines from the junctions of the diamonds in the sketch (c).

★ Measure the distance between the lines. Add this measurement to two sides of the 1½" 45° diamond (d). The diamond now measures one additional row wider but all angles remain the same and the sides are equal.

★ Measure the diamond from tip to tip (e).

★ Draw a circle using the tip to tip measurement. Draw a line through the middle of the circle. Draw a second line through the middle of the circle at a right angle to the first line (f).

★ Place a tracing of the diamond in the circle.

★ Place a second diamond opposite to make a diamond pair. Draw a line from star tip to star tip. (g)

★ Measure from the circle center to the line at the tips to find half of the size of the square. Double the measurement to find the square that will fit around the star (h).

★ Trace or redraft the star within the newly established square with the size of the feathers pre-determined without math.

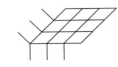

c. draw right angles

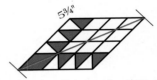

d. make squares equal to the distance between the right angle lines on two sides

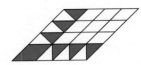

e. measure the distance from tip to tip

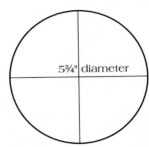

f. draw a circle and divide into quarters

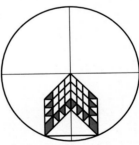

g. place a pair of diamonds with tips at center of circle; draw a line from tip to tip.

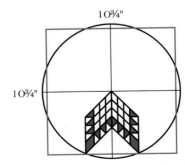

h. double the tip to tip measurement to find the size of square to fit around star

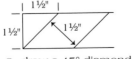

a. draw a 45° diamond

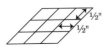

b. divide diamond into equal smaller diamonds

Fig. 9–5a–h. Fuss-free feathers for the octagon star

MONTANA FEATHERED STAR, 52" x 52", made by Diane Jenks.

MONTANA FEATHERED STAR
52" x 52"

1 Giant Sawtooth Star
4 Anvil Blocks, 4"
12 Half-Anvil Blocks, 4" x 6"

★ ★ ★

half-squares
p. 152

Materials	Yds.	First cut		Second cut	
Lt. blue	1¼	1 rectangle	18" x 42"	bias half-squares	
		3 strips	3¼"	28 squares	3¼"
		1 rectangle	9" x 42"	1 square	9"
		2 squares	7¼"		
		2 squares	5¼"		
		6 squares	4⅛"		
		8 squares	1⅞"		
Dk. blue	2⅛	1 rectangle	18" x 42"	bias half-squares	
		2 strips	3¼"	20 squares	3¼"
		2 strips	1½"	(see page 152)	
		1 strip	1½"	16 squares	1½"
		1 rectangle	9" x 42"	2 squares	9"
				1 square	6½"
				4 squares	2⅞"
BORDERS		5 strips	5½"		
Lt. purple	¼	2 strips	2⅞"	16 squares	2⅞"
Dk. purple	⅜	1 square	7¼"		
		4 squares	6½"		
Red	⅜	1 strip	1⅞"	8 squares	1⅞"
		1 square	9"		
		4 squares	2½"		
Aqua	1	1 square	21¼"		
		4 squares	10½"		
Backing	3⅜	2 panels	28½" x 56"		
Binding	½				
Batting		56" x 56"			

Cut strips selvage to selvage. Be sure to label all your pieces with their cut sizes.

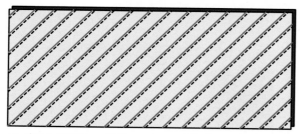

a. draw 45° lines 1⅞" apart; sew ¼" from drawn line

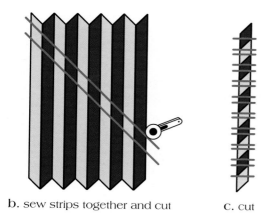

b. sew strips together and cut   c. cut

Fig. 9–6a–c. Bias-strip squares

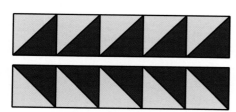

a. sew five half-squares together

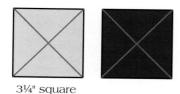

3¼" square

b. cut squares twice diagonally

c. cut mirror-image pairs of star tips

Fig. 9–7a–c. Corner setting-square units

Sewing

MONTANA FEATHERED STAR is a giant feathered Sawtooth Star with a grid of four Feathered Stars, on point, inside it. Two different techniques are used to make the half-squares: the half-square and the bias-square. Care must be used to maintain the mirror-image half-squares.

UNIT ASSEMBLY

Large half-squares

★ Use the 18" x 42" light blue and dark blue rectangles to make 112 half-squares by using a bias-strip method (Fig. 9–6a–c). The bias lines are 1⅞" apart. Cut a total of 112 of the larger half-squares.

★ Trim all the squares by using the half-square template made from the full-size pattern on page 153. Be sure to align the diagonal line on the template with the diagonal seam lines on the half-squares.

Corner setting-square units

★ Sew five half-squares together in a row (Fig. 9–7a). Make eight rows like Fig. 9–7a. Sew 8 mirror image rows. Set the remaining half-squares aside for now.

★ Cut the 28 3¼" light blue squares twice diagonally to make 112 quarter-square triangles (b).

★ Cut the 20 3¼" dark blue squares twice diagonally to make 80 quarter-square triangles for large triangle stops (b).

★ Make a star-tip template from the full-size pattern on page 154. Place two dark blue 1½" strips right sides together. Use the template to cut eight mirror-image pairs of star tips from from two strips, right sides together (c).

★ To help you sew the pieces together in the correct orientation, lay the four 10½" aqua corner setting squares on a flat surface in the positions they will occupy in the quilt.

★ Position two half-square rows on adjacent sides of each setting square as shown in (d). Place a light blue quarter-square triangle, hereafter called a "triangle stop," in position at the end of each row.

★ Place a dark blue quarter-square triangle between the half-square rows. These triangles at the junction of the two feather rows will be referred to as "peak triangles." Place the star tips in position, paying careful attention to their orientation.

★ Sew the half-square rows, stops, peaks, and star tips together as shown in (e). Sew the rows to the setting squares (f).

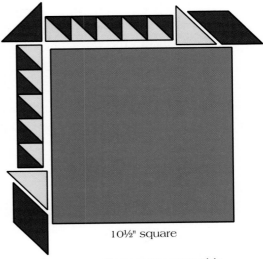

10½" square

d. corner setting-square assembly

e. sew the feather units together

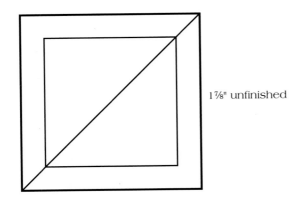

1⅞" unfinished

Full-size half-square template pattern

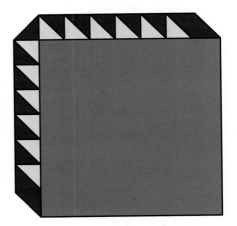

f. sew the rows to the setting square

Fig. 9–7d–f. Corner setting-square units.

a. rectangle units

7¼" square   7¼" square

b. cut squares diagonally twice to make base triangles

3⅛" square   2¼" square
peak triangle   stop triangle

stop triangle   peak

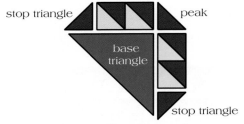

base
triangle

stop triangle

c. sew the units together

2⅞" square

d. cut square diagonally for star-point corners

base
triangle

e. sew half-squares to complete the rectangle unit

Fig. 9–8a–e. Rectangle units

Rectangle units: There are eight rectangle units with light blue base triangles and four rectangle units with dark purple base triangles (Fig. 9–8a).

★ To make the base triangles, cut the one dark purple and the two light blue 7¼" squares diagonally twice like an X (b).

★ For the units' feather rows, sew 24 mirror image sets of two half-squares. Place light blue triangle stops at the ends of the rows. Add the dark blue peaks in between.

★ Sew the half-square rows, stops, and peaks together as shown in (c). Sew the rows to the base triangles.

★ Cut the 16 2⅞" light purple squares diagonally once (d). These half-square triangles will become the star points of the four Feathered Stars on point, secondary designs within the giant Sawtooth Star.

★ Sew two light purple half-square triangles to each unit to complete the rectangle units (e). Set the remaining light purple triangles aside.

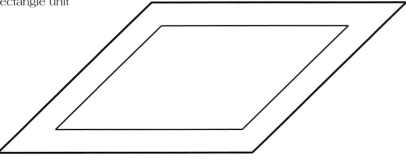

Full-size star-tip template pattern

Small half-squares

★ Place the light blue and dark blue 9" squares right sides together. Draw a grid of 2" squares on the back of the light blue fabric. Draw the diagonals of the squares. Sew seams ¼" on both sides of the drawn diagonals. Cut the squares apart on the square grid lines and on the diagonal lines. Re-cut the 16 oversized squares to 1½" (Fig. 9–9a–b).

★ Repeat for the dark blue and the red 9" squares to make the small half-squares for the red Anvil blocks.

Half-anvil/star-point units

★ Cut the two 4⅛" light blue squares diagonally twice to make eight base triangles (Fig. 9–10a).

★ Cut the eight 1⅞" light blue squares in half diagonally to make the stops for the feather rows (b).

★ Sew the small light blue/dark blue half-squares, stops, and 1½" dark blue squares in rows as shown in (c). Sew the rows to the light blue base triangles to make eight half-anvil blocks.

★ Cut four 4⅛" light blue squares diagonally once to make eight right-angle triangles (d).

★ Sew the light blue right-angle triangles to the half-anvil blocks as shown in (e, page 156). Notice that there are four "left" and four "right" half-anvil units.

★ To make the remaining feather rows for the star-point units, sew two light blue and two dark blue quarter-square triangles (already cut from 3¼" squares) as shown in (f, page 156).

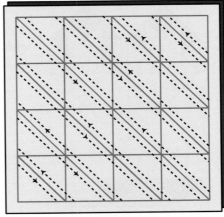

9" square

a. sew ¼" seams on both sides of diagonals; cut on all drawn lines

b. trim half-squares to 1½"

Fig. 9–9a–b. Small half-squares

4⅛" square

a. make base triangles

1⅞" square

b. cut squares diagonally for "stop" triangle

c. sew half-anvil block together

4⅛" square

d. cut squares diagonally to make right-angle triangle

Fig. 9–10a–d. Half-anvil units

e. stitch right-angle triangles to the half-anvil blocks

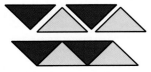

f. sew diagonal feather rows (four are mirror images)

g. sew the pieced row to the base triangle

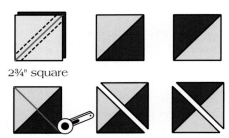

2¾" square

h. make half-square triangles, cut on opposite diagonal

i. sew two-color triangle to the half-anvil unit

Fig. 9–11a–d. Half-anvil units, continued

★ Sew the pieced rows to the base triangles of the half-anvil units (g).

★ Sew light blue and dark blue 2¾" squares together to make half-squares. Cut once on the opposite diagonal to make two-color triangles. (h).

★ Sew the two-color triangles to the half-anvil units, four of which are mirror image (i).

★ Sew the short side of each of the remaining 2⅞" light purple half-square triangles to the appropriate side of the half-anvil unit to complete four right and four left Sawtooth Star point units (j).

Anvil blocks

★ Sew the small red/dark blue half-squares, stops, and dark blue 1 ½" squares together as shown in Fig. 9–12a.

★ Sew the remaining dark blue 2⅞" half-square triangles to the sides of the anvils to complete the Anvil blocks (b).

j. sew half-square triangle to complete the half-anvil/star-point unit

Feathered Star centers

★ Sew two rectangle units that have light blue base triangles to opposite sides of four of the dark purple 6½" squares.

★ Sew two rectangle units that have purple base triangles to opposite sides of one dark blue 6½" square (see assembly diagram)). Set aside the remaining two rectangle units.

QUILT ASSEMBLY

★ Assemble the wallhanging in three sections, a diagonal row and two large triangles.

★ Sew two star-point units to each corner setting square and add the pieces containing the rectangle units.

★ Cut the 21¼" aqua squares diagonally twice to make the side triangles. Add side triangles to two of the star-point/rectangle pieces. To make the large triangle sections, add background base triangle fabric to two feathered corners to make the large triangle units. (Fig. 9–13a)

★ Sew two anvil blocks to each remaining rectangle unit and add these to the center square piece as shown (b, page 158).

★ Sew two star-point pieces to the center unit to complete the diagonal section, then sew the three sections of the quilt together.

a. anvil block

b. sew half-square triangles to sides of the anvils

Fig. 9–12a–b. Anvil blocks

a. assemble the corner triangle units

Fig. 9–13a. Quilt assembly

Border 1

★ Join the 5 border strips, end to end, with bias seams as needed to create the border lengths.

★ Sew the border strips to the quilt and miter the corners.

Border 2

★ Join the remaining half-squares into eight rows. Each row will contain 17 left and 17 right half-squares. Sew two of the rows to opposite sides of the quilt.

★ Cut the four 2⅞" light blue squares to size by using a template made from pattern B.

★ Sew a light blue square to each end of the two remaining rows of half-squares and sew these rows to the quilt (Fig. 9–14).

FINISHING

Layer the quilt with batting and a backing, then quilt the layers. Bind the raw edges of the quilt with 2" continuous, double-fold bias binding.

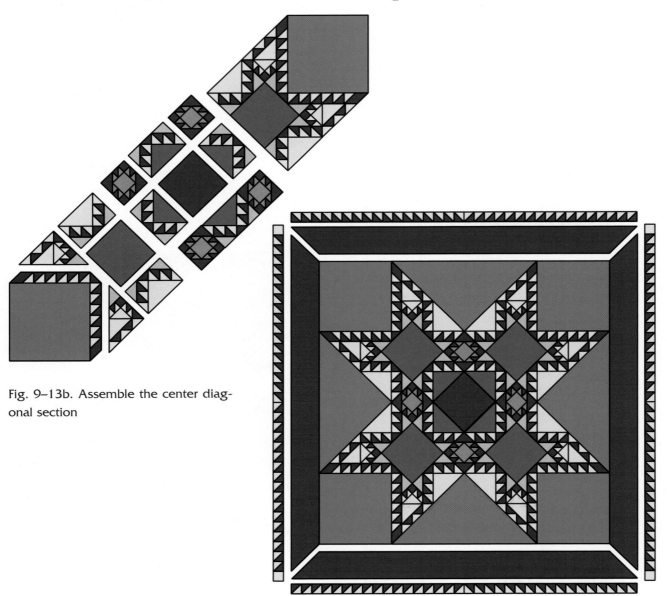

Fig. 9–13b. Assemble the center diagonal section

Fig. 9–14. Quilt assembly

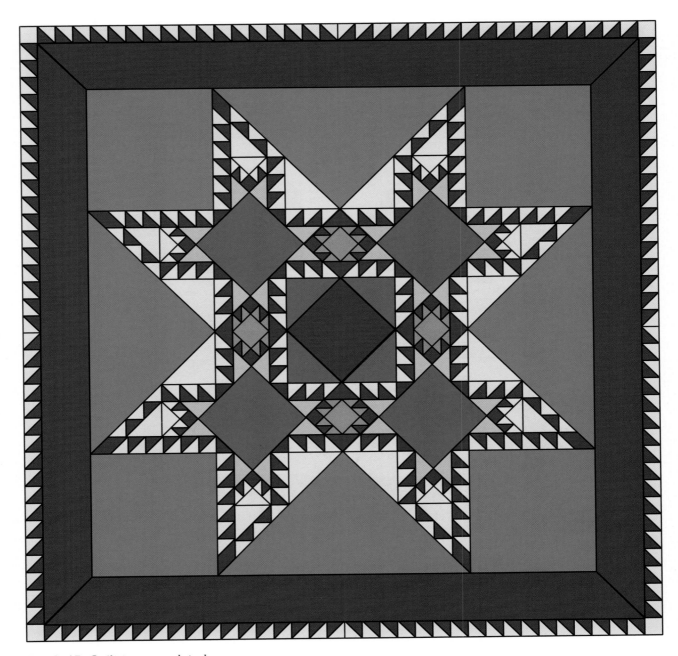

Fig. 9–15. Quilt top completed

SNOW CRYSTALS, 33" x 33", made by Mary Ann Wattam.

Chapter 10

Specialized Technique for Clusters of Stars – Multiple Star Points

In this technique, the star points begin as borders of a Square-Within-a-Square. The use of the background square to perfectly align and sew the mitered star points makes the blocks fast and easy.

Jackson Star

Carpenter's Wheel

Double Peony

Dutch Rose

Fig. 10–1a–d.

EASY WEDGE-PIECED STAR POINTS

This technique would be appropriate for several star blocks, for instance, the Jackson Star, also known as Four Stars, a four-star block design. The star points are parallelograms. Also appropriate are octagon-based stars such as Carpenter's Wheel, Double Peony, and Dutch Rose. (Fig. 10–1a–d)

★ Cut strips of fabric equal to the width of the star point plus seam allowances.

★ Use a wedge-shaped template (Fig. 10–2a) to cut wedge-shaped pieces from each strip (b).

★ Place a wedge, right sides together, in the corner of a square. Match the slanted edges of the wedge with the sides of the square. Starting and ending ¼" from the edge, sew the wedges to the background square (c). Do not cut away the waste triangle.

★ Place the next wedge on the opposite corner. Sew in place as before (d).

★ Make a template of the corner to position wedges 3 and 4.

★ The remaining two wedges require aid in positioning because the edges of the square aren't visible. Fold the third and fourth wedges in half and finger press a center mark. Use the corner template to position

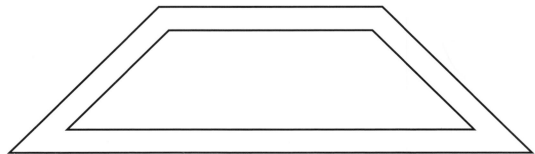

Fig. 10–2a. Full-sized wedge for star points

the third and fourth wedges. Sew the wedges to the square on point within the background square.

★ To sew the seams between the wedges, fold the square back on itself, right sides together. Pin the two corners of the square together.

★ Sew the wedge tips from the outside to the square (e). Refold the background square three more times to sew the remaining miters.

★ Press the block from the back and from the front. Press the seams at the miters counter clockwise (f).

★ Turn the squares face down on the cutting mat. Cut the wedges on opposite sides even with the square (g).

★ Turn the blocks face up. Lift each wedge to cut away the corners of the square (h).

The secret to this technique

☆ ☆ ☆

The wedges automatically position themselves. No match marks. The square folded in half perfectly aligns the wedges. No pins. Using a wedge instead of diamonds means no bias diamond edges to stitch.

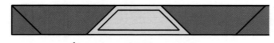

b. cut wedge from strips

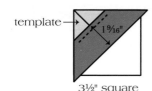

template → 1 9/16"

3½" square

c. align wedge with edges of square; make a corner template to align final two wedges

Fig. 10–2b–c. Easy wedge-pieced star points

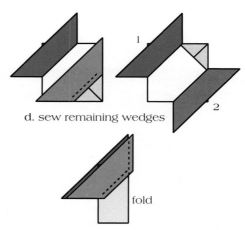

1
2

d. sew remaining wedges

fold

e. match the wedges and sew the corners

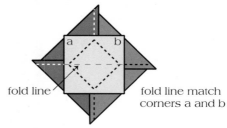

a   b

fold line   fold line match
                     corners a and b

f. press the miters clockwise

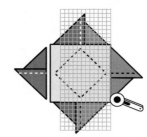

g. cut two opposite wedges using the edge of square as a guide

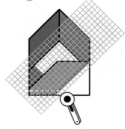

h. trim the corners of the square

i. wedge unit

Fig. 10–2c–i. Easy wedge-pieced star points

RUSSIAN THISTLES, 88" x 100", made by Beaver Aspevig.

RUSSIAN THISTLES
88" x 100"

14 Jackson Star Blocks, 12"

★ ★ ★
**easy
wedge-pieced
star-points**
p. 167

★ ★ ★
**strip-pieced
star-points**
p. 168

Cut strips selvage to selvage. Be sure to label all your pieces with their cut sizes.

Materials	Yds.	First cut		Second cut	
Background	8¼				
CENTER PANEL		1 rectangle	24½" x 36½"		
BORDER 1		4 strips	12½" x 36½"		
		2 strips	12½" x 60½"		
JOINING STRIPS		4 strips	6½" x 36½"		
STRIPS BELOW BASE TRIANGLE					
		4 strips	2½" x 36½"		
		1 square	18¼"		
BLOCKS & PIECED BORDERS		11 strips	4¼"	92 squares	4¼"
		6 strips	3½"	70 squares	3½"
		6 strips	2½"	strip piecing star-points slices	
		5 strips	2"	56 rectangles	2" x 3½"
		15 strips	2"	296 squares	2"
Medium color	1⅞				
BIAS BINDING		1 rectangle	18" x 42"		
STAR POINTS		8 strips	2¹⁄₁₆"	strip piecing star-points slices	
		12 strips	*1⁹⁄₁₆"	wedges	
Dark color	1⅞				
BORDER 2		10 strips	2½"		
STAR POINTS		8 strips	2¹⁄₁₆"	strip piecing star-points slices	
		12 strips	*1⁹⁄₁₆"	wedges	
Bias binding	½ yard included in medium color				
Backing	9	3 panels	one – 42" x 96"	two – 27" x 96"	
Batting	96" x 108"				

*A ruler marked in sixteenths is recommended.

3½" square

a. make a wedge guide

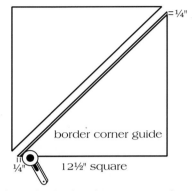

= ¼"

border corner guide

¼"   12½" square

b. make the border corner guide

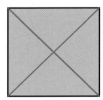

4¼" square

c. cut square diagonally twice to make base triangles

Fig. 10–3a–c. Preparations for star points

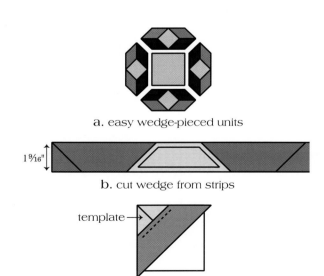

a. easy wedge-pieced units

1 ⁹⁄₁₆"

b. cut wedge from strips

template →

3½" square

c. align wedge with edges of square; make a corner template to align wedges

Fig. 10–4a–c. Wedge-pieced star points

Preparation

Make a template for the wedge shape to make cutting the pieces fast and easy. The border corner guide positions the wedges for stitching.

JACKSON STAR BLOCKS

Template

★ For the easy wedge-cut star points, which are used in the center of 14 Russian Thistle blocks, trace the wedge pattern (page 162) on paper. Cut out the paper wedge and paste it to template plastic. Cut out the plastic template.

Wedge guide

★ Cut a 3½" square from paper. Place the wedge template in the corner of the square so that both ends of the wedge are even with the sides of the square. Cut away and keep the triangle as a positioning guide. Fold the paper triangle in half to mark the center (Fig. 10–3a).

Border corner guide

★ Draw a 12½" square on paper. Cut the square in half diagonally. Cut away ¼" from the long side of one of the triangles (b).

Base triangles

★ Cut the 92 4¼" background squares diagonally twice, in an X, to make 368 base triangles for the blocks and pieced border (c).

Sewing

The center portion of each block will be made with wedge units (Fig. 10–4a). The star points at the edge of the blocks and those at the edge of the quilt will be strip pieced.

BLOCK ASSEMBLY

Easy wedge-pieced star points

★ Use the wedge template to cut 112 wedges from the 1⁹⁄₁₆" medium strips and 112 wedges from the 1⁹⁄₁₆" dark strips (b).

★ Place a dark color wedge in the corner of a 3½" square of background fabric. Slide the wedge away from the corner until the 45° angled ends of the wedge are even with the sides of the square. Repeat with a second wedge.

★ Starting and ending ¼" from the edges, sew across the wedge (c). Do not cut away the waste triangle. Sew the medium color wedge opposite the first corner.

★ Fold a second dark color wedge in half and finger press a center mark to use as a placement guide. Use the wedge guide to position the second dark wedge, and sew it in place (d). Sew a medium color for the fourth wedge.

★ To join the corners of the wedges, fold the square back on itself, wrong sides together, and pin. Sew the wedge tips from the outside edge toward the square (e).

★ Press the block from the back and from the front. Press the seams of the 45° angles counterclockwise (f). Repeat the sewing and pressing for 56 squares. Set the remainder of the 3½" squares aside.

★ Turn the squares face down on the cutting mat. Align the ruler with the edge of the square to cut away one dark and one medium corner (g). Trim all 56 squares with wedge borders.

★ Turn the units face up. Lift each

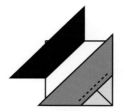

d. sew remaining wedges

e. match the wedges and sew the corners

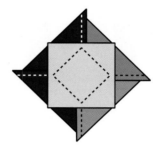

f. press the miters clockwise

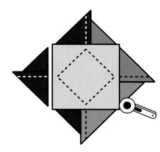

g. cut two opposite wedges using the edge of square as a guide

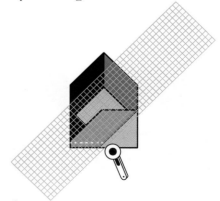

h. trim the corners of the square

Fig. 10–4d-h. Wedge-pieced star points

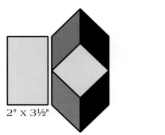

2" x 3½"

a. sew a rectangle to each wedge unit

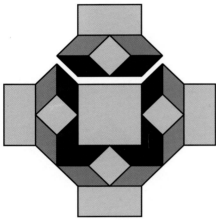

b. sew the units to the center square

Fig. 10–5a–b. Wedge-pieced star points, block assembly

wedge and cut away the corners of the original square (h, page 167) leaving a ¼" seam allowance.

BLOCK ASSEMBLY

★ Beginning and ending ¼" from the edge, sew a 2" x 3½" background rectangle to the medium color edges of each of the wedge units (Fig. 10–5a).

★ Place four wedge units around a center 3½" background square with the dark color edges facing the square. Sew the units to the square as shown in the block assembly diagram (b). Miter the wedge units at the corners to create half stars.

★ With the tip of the iron, lightly press the seams of the center square and the surrounding squares flat. Press all dark color star-point seam allowances in a counterclockwise direction. Make 14 of these partial blocks, then set aside.

STRIP-PIECED STAR POINTS

★ Strip-pieced star points will be cut from pairs of 2⅟₁₆" strips sewn on one long edge (Fig. 10–6a). Do not press the strips open. Make the following pairs of strips: 3 background strip sets; 4 medium color strip sets, 1 dark strip set, and 10 medium/dark strip sets.

★ Slice the strip pairs with 45° degree cuts every 1⁹⁄₁₆" to make 44 star-point pairs from the background strips, 172 pairs from the medium strips, 8 star pairs from the dark strips.

★ From the medium/dark strips, cut 72 star pairs from right to left and 72 from left to right. (Keep the seam on the top so that an equal

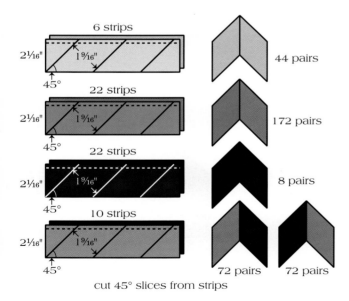

6 strips
2⅟₁₆"   1⁹⁄₁₆"   44 pairs
45°

22 strips
2⅟₁₆"   1⁹⁄₁₆"   172 pairs
45°

22 strips
2⅟₁₆"   1⁹⁄₁₆"   8 pairs
45°

10 strips
2⅟₁₆"   1⁹⁄₁₆"
45°   72 pairs   72 pairs

cut 45° slices from strips

Fig. 10–6. Strip-pieced star points

number of mirror-image star-point pairs will be cut.)

Block assembly:

★ Sew pairs of medium color star points to base triangles, as follows:

★ Finger press the star-point pairs open. Pick out the stitches in the seam allowance at the intersection of the star points (Fig. 10–7a). Align one of the star points, right sides together, with the base triangle's 45° angle. Sew from the angle to the peak of the triangle. Continue stitching the second star point to the base triangle from the peak to the 45° angle of the base triangle (b).

★ Sew all the star-point pairs to base triangles to complete these units (b).

★ Stitch two medium color base triangle units to adjacent sides of 56 2" background squares to make half stars. Stitch the star points together as if mitering a border corner (c).

★ Use the tip of the iron to press the mitered seam allowances clockwise. (The seam allowances should be pressed in the opposite direction to those pressed previously so that the seams in the center of the star can be matched easily.)

★ Position a star half in one corner of a partial block, right sides together. Use a pin to match the star half seams in the center. Stitch four basting stitches across the center seams. Stop and check the accuracy of the center seams.

★ Begin and end ¼" from the edge of the corners of the square. Stitch seam.

★ Take the block from beneath the presser foot. Reposition the block to match the star half to a 2" x 3½"

a. pick out stitches at intersection

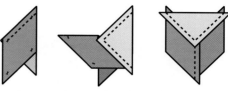

b. sew diamond to the base triangle

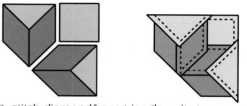

c. stitch diamond/base-triangle units to squares

d. sew the half stars to corners of center

e. Jackson Stars block

Fig. 10–6a–e. Block assembly

a.
make 4
6 dark points
2 medium points

b.
make 44
4 medium points
2 dark points
2 background points

c.
make 8
6 medium points
2 dark points

d.
make 16
2 medium points
2 dark points

Fig. 10–8. Star blocks for border

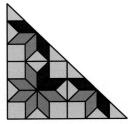

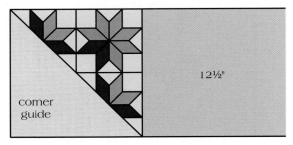

a. sew one block and two half-blocks for corner unit

corner
guide

12½"

b. butt corner unit to the corner guide; stitch
to border strip

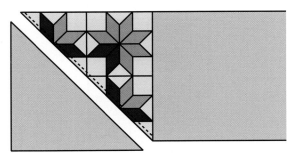

c. trim corner of background

Fig. 10–9a–c. Border stars, corner triangles

background rectangle. Sew from
the seam that joins the star halves
to the edge of the block.

★ Sew the other side of the star half
to the adjacent rectangle in the
same manner. Finish the block by
setting in the three remaining star
halves (d, page 169). Complete all
14 blocks (e, page 169).

QUILT CENTER ASSEMBLY

★ Sew three 12½" Thistle blocks together in a row for one side of the
24½" x 36½" background rectangle
(Fig. 10–11). Sew three blocks together for the opposite side. Sew
the blocks to the long sides of the
rectangle.

★ Sew four Thistle blocks together for
the top and four for the bottom of
the quilt center. Sew the rows to
the top and bottom to complete
the quilt center.

BORDER 1

★ Measure the quilt center. It should
be 48½" x 60½".

★ Sew two 12½" x 60½" background
strips to the sides of the center.

★ Sew two 12½" x 36½" strips end to
end for the quilt top and again to
the bottom. (The center seam
becomes a guide for the mid-point
triangles.)

BORDER STARS

There are three different star blocks and a
half star block for the borders. Refer to the
star blocks for borders to make 4 A blocks,
44 B's, 8 C's, and 16 D's (Fig. 10–8). Cut 8 3⅜"
squares diagonally twice to make triangles.

Corner triangles

★ Make four pieced triangles as shown in Fig. 10–9a.

★ Place the border corner guide in one corner of the 12½" border. Butt a pieced triangle, right sides together, against the long side of the paper triangle. Sew the pieced triangle to the end (b). Cut away the background fabric (c). Repeat these steps to replace the remaining three corners with pieced triangles.

Border strips

★ The star borders at the top and bottom of the quilt have three B star blocks at each end with a 6½" x 36½" joining strip in the middle. The side borders have four B star blocks at each end with the same size joining strip in the middle. Sew a Block A to each end of the side borders with the medium points toward the enter of the quilt. Make the border strips as described and sew them to the quilt center as shown in the quilt assembly diagram (Fig. 10–10).

★ Note: the remaining stars at the midpoint of each side are pieced as a triangular unit and appliquéd to the quilt.

Mid-point star unit

★ Cut the 18¼" background square twice like an X to make four base triangles for the mid-point star units.

★ Sew four mid-point star units as shown in Fig. 10–11.

★ Center and sew the 2½" x 36½" strips of background fabric to the bottom of each mid-point triangle.

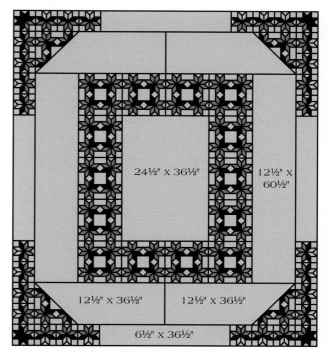

24½" x 36½"

12½" x 60½"

12½" x 36½"   12½" x 36½"

6½" x 36½"

Fig. 10–10. Quilt assembly

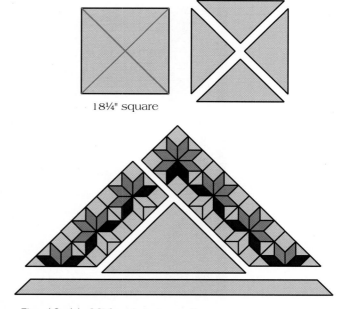

18¼" square

Fig. 10–11. Mid-point star unit

★ To create a guide line for turning under the allowances, machine stitch ¼" in from the edge on two sides of each mid-point star unit. Using the the stitched line as a guide, press the seam allowance under.

★ Appliqué each mid-point star unit in place on the four sides of the quilt.

★ Leaving a ¼" seam allowance, trim away the background fabric beneath the appliquéd triangles.

BORDER 3

★ Use the 10 2½" dark color strips, sewn end to end with a bias seam, to make the final border for the quilt.

★ Sew the 2" borders to the quilt and miter the corners.

FINISHING

Layer the quilt with batting and backing and quilt as desired. Bind the raw edges of the quilt with 2" continuous, double-fold bias binding.

Fig. 10–12. Completed quilt top

Bibliography

Beyer, Jinny, *The Quilter's Album of Blocks and Borders*, EPM Publications, Inc., McLean, Virginia, 1980.

Bradkin, Cheryl Greider, *The Seminole Patchwork Book*, Yours Truly, Inc., Atlanta, 1980.

Duerstock, Judy, "*Quick Piecing Half-Square Triangles*," Quilter's Newsletter Magazine (July/August 1998): 48-49.

Finley, Ruth E., *Old Patchwork Quilts and the Women Who Made Them*, Charles T. Branford, Co., Newton Center, Massachusetts, 1929.

Flynn, John, *Feathered Sun*, Flynn Quilt Frame Co., Billings, Montana, 56 pp.

Hall, Carrie A. and Rose G. Kretsinger, *The Romance of the Patchwork Quilt in America*, Bonanza Books, A Division of Crown Publishers, New York, 1935.

Hughes, Trudie, *Template-Free Quiltmaking*, That Patchwork Place, Bothell, Washington, 1986.

Johannah, Barbara, *The Quick Quiltmaking Handbook*, Pride of the Forest Press, Menlo Park, California, 1979.

Leman, Bonnie and Judy Martin, *Log Cabin Quilts*, Moon Over the Mountain Publishing Co., Wheat Ridge, Colorado. 1980.

_____. *Taking the Math Out of Making Patchwork Quilts*, Moon Over the Mountain Publishing Co., Wheat Ridge, Colorado, 1981.

Martin, Nancy J., *Back to Square One*, That Patchwork Place, Bothell, Washington, 1988.

Mathieson, Judy, *Mariner's Compass, An American Quilt Classic*, C & T Publishing, Lafayette, California, 1987.

McCloskey, Marsha, *Feathered Star Quilts*, That Patchwork Place, Bothell, Washington, 1987.

Mills, Susan Winter, *Illustrated Index to Traditional American Quilt Patterns*, Arco Publishing, New York, 1980.

Parker, Linda, *Montana Star Quilts*, Montana Quilts, Helena, Montana, 1997.

Young, Blanche and Helen, *The Lone Star Quilt Handbook*, Oak View, California, 1979.

Index

About the Author

After graduating from Concordia College in Moorhead, Minnesota, Gail taught English in the Minneapolis Public Schools. A gift of quilt blocks made from old worn fabrics, a magazine article, and a 1963 purchase of a needlework book by Rose Wilder Lane were the beginnings of her quiltmaking journey.

Gail learned about quilts and quiltmaking by reading books. Her study of quiltmaking grew coincidentally with raising three active daughters. Winning a sweepstakes award at a local fair led to teaching adult education quilting classes. In 1982 Gail was certified as a national quilting teacher by the Embroiderer's Guild of America. Her quilts have been shown locally and juried into regional quilt shows.

In *Sew Many Stars*, Gail gathers together many quick-piecing techniques and adds her own new methods for rotary cutting, short-cut methods to give others the time required to finish their quilts and be able to wrap them around their children and their dreams.

Gail and her recently-retired husband live 36 miles from the Canadian border in a small town on the prairies of Montana near where her parents raised wheat and where her grandparents homesteaded.

Other AQS Books

This is only a small selection of the books available from the American Quilter's Society. AQS books are known worldwide for timely topics, clear writing, beautiful color photos, and accurate illustrations and patterns. The following books are available from your local bookseller, quilt shop, or public library.

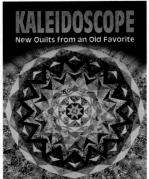

#5296 $16.95

#4898 $16.95

#5589 $21.95

#4545 $18.95

#4995 $19.95

#5339 $19.95

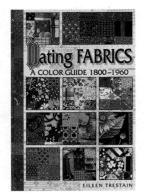

#4827 (6" x 9") $24.95

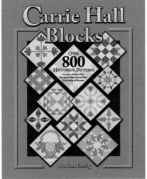

#4957 (HB) $34.95

#5210 $18.95